DATE DUE

JAN 27 2011	
SEP 2 8 2012	

The Music Library

The History of
World Music

By Stuart A. Kallen

LUCENT BOOKS

An imprint of Thomson Gale, a part of The Thomson Corporation

THOMSON

GALE

Detroit • New York • San Francisco • San Diego • New Haven, Conn. • Waterville, Maine • London • Munich

For more information, contact
Lucent Books
27500 Drake Rd.
Farmington Hills, MI 48331-3535
Or you can visit our Internet site at http://www.gale.com

LIBRARY OF CONGRESS CATALOGING-IN-PUBLICATION DATA

Kallen, Stuart A., 1955–
 The history of world music / by Stuart A. Kallen.
  p. cm. — (The music library)
 Includes bibliographical references (p.   ) and index.
 ISBN 1-59018-741-5 (hard cover : alk. paper) 1. World music—History and criticism—Juvenile literature. I. Title. II. Series: Music library (San Diego, Calif.)
ML3928.K355 2006
780'.9—dc22
                                                                        2005021584

Printed in the United States of America

• Contents •

• Foreword •

In the nineteenth century, English novelist Charles Kingsley wrote, "Music speaks straight to our hearts and spirits, to the very core and root of our souls. . . . Music soothes us, stirs us up . . . melts us to tears." As Kingsley stated, music is much more than just a pleasant arrangement of sounds. It is the resonance of emotion, a joyful noise, a human endeavor that can soothe the spirit or excite the soul. Musicians can also imitate the expressive palate of the earth, from the violent fury of a hurricane to the gentle flow of a babbling brook.

The word *music* is derived from the fabled Greek muses, the children of Apollo who ruled the realms of inspiration and imagination. Composers have long called upon the muses for help and insight. Music is not merely the result of emotions and pleasurable sensations, however.

Music is a discipline subject to formal study and analysis. It involves the juxtaposition of creative elements such as rhythm, melody, and harmony with intellectual aspects of composition, theory, and instrumentation. Like painters mixing red, blue, and yellow into thousands of colors, musicians blend these various elements to create classical symphonies, jazz improvisations, country ballads, and rock-and-roll tunes.

Throughout centuries of musical history, individual musical elements have been blended and modified in infinite ways. The resulting sounds may convey a whole range of moods, emotions, reactions, and messages. Music, then, is both an expression and reflection of human experience and emotion.

The foundations of modern musical styles were laid down by the first ancient musicians who used wood, rocks, animal skins—and their own bodies—to re-create the sounds of the natural world in which they lived. With their hands, their feet, and their very breath they ignited the passions of listeners and moved them to their feet. The dancing, in turn, had a mesmerizing and hypnotic effect that allowed people to transcend their worldly concerns. Through music they could achieve a level of shared experience that could not be found in other forms of communication. For this reason, music has always been part of religious endeavors, from ancient Egyptian religious ceremonies to modern Christian masses. And it has inspired dance movements from kings and queens spinning the minuet to punk rockers slamming together in a mosh pit.

By examining musical genres ranging from Western classical music to rock and roll, readers will find a new understanding of old music and develop an appreciation for new sounds. Books in Lucent's Music Library focus on the music, the musicians, the instruments, and on music's place in cultural history. The songs and artists examined may be easily found in the CD and sheet music collections of local libraries so that readers may study and enjoy the music covered in the books. Informative sidebars, annotated bibliographies, and complete indexes highlight the text in each volume and provide young readers with many opportunities for further discussion and research.

Billions of Listeners Worldwide

The sounds collectively known as world music are as old as human culture and as new as the latest dance record from Brazil. World music, loosely defined as the music of indigenous people throughout the world, may be played in a traditional manner dating back centuries or updated and played on modern instruments such as electric guitars, synthesizers, and drum kits. It can be referred to as homegrown, roots, international, or ethnic music. No matter how it is labeled, the style is often linked to traditional cultures from which a particular musical genre has evolved. Its places of origin include Africa, the Middle East, the Far East, India, South and Central America, the Caribbean, and even the United States, where Native Americans, Louisiana Cajuns, and others contribute to the sounds collectively known as world music.

What was once considered regional music now spans the globe. This has resulted in a cross-pollination of styles in which, for example, African drum music inspires Jamaican reggae artists whose musical beat is adapted by Hawaiian musicians. Traditional Peruvian bands are heard on the central squares of eastern European towns, while infectious Puerto Rican dance music is the hottest trend in the clubs of Manhattan.

Even though this global community of musicians promotes an abundance of musical genres, most world music stars rarely appear on music television, and their music is not often played by commercial radio stations. In fact, world music did not exist as a distinct musical genre until a few owners of small London record companies invented the category in 1987. At that time, creative and innovative sounds from Africa, Latin America, eastern Europe, and elsewhere could not easily be sold in record stores because they did not conveniently fit into traditional musical categories such as rock, country, jazz, or classical. To counter this problem, the record executives instituted a month-long campaign to promote their sounds to record buyers, music critics, and store owners. To make the job easier, the disparate sounds from the four corners of the globe were placed under a single name, world music. While the marketing campaign was short, the name *world music* stuck.

Before long, sounds tagged world music found their place in record stores, music magazines, and books. In 1990 the music industry magazine *Billboard* introduced its world music chart to track sales of albums from Africa to the Americas that fit into the broadly defined category. Within a few months, this chart showed that world music was the fastest growing segment of the record business and that the music was finding new listeners every day. In the twenty-first century, thanks to satellite and Web radio stations and the availability of world music CDs on the Internet and at public libraries, the genre is more popular than ever. And every day countless extremely talented people create exceptional music throughout the world.

These Lithuanian folk dancers are keeping their musical traditions alive.

World music encompasses a broad range of indigenous cultural traditions, such as Hawaiian music and dance.

Besides being a force in its own right, world music has inspired hundreds of rock and rap musicians. It has been incorporated into songs by bar bands, record producers, and superstars. Regional sounds from places as diverse as Louisiana, Jamaica, and Africa have had a lasting impact on rock and roll, jazz, and even country music.

"Enter Other Places and Stay There"

The history of world music is, in a sense, the history of the world and its people. In many places, such as Africa, South and Central America, and the Middle East, musicians sing about war, poverty, despotic governments, and other influences in their lives. Lyrics reflect the emotions, desires, and experiences of those who have shaped a nation or a region. The songs have inspired people to love, rebel, seek peace, or simply sing and dance. And while this music originates in dissimilar cultures and is sung in dozens of different languages, it often has a unifying effect.

People in nations thousands of miles away can appreciate the beauty, passions, and wonders of a foreign culture without ever leaving home. And song offers a way for people to recognize their common humanity. Even without understanding the language of the singer, a listener can relate to him or her through melody, rhythm, and emotion. As experimental rock musician Brian Eno writes in *Rhythm Planet:*

> World Music invites you to enter other places and stay there for a while. . . . Listening to such music broadens the number of possible worlds . . . that you can inhabit in your mind. . . . [It] is really a way of exercising this basic ability to imagine and participate in other worlds, to enjoy their logic and balance, to see why things are the way they are within them.[1]

Chapter One

Music of Southern Africa

Africa is the second largest continent on earth and is thought to be the birthplace of the human race. This five thousand-mile-long landmass (8,047km) is populated by more than 300 million people who divide themselves into three thousand different ethnic groups. More than one thousand distinct indigenous languages are spoken in Africa. In this multicul-

tural milieu, it is little wonder that Africans produce a wide array of unique music.

While Africans participate in thousands of different traditions, they also share many musical characteristics. For example, in the southern African nations of Zimbabwe, South Africa, and Mozambique, as is true elsewhere in Africa, drums are central to music, as

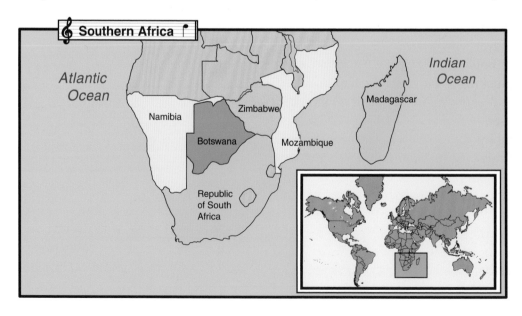

Southern Africa

Atlantic Ocean

Indian Ocean

Namibia

Zimbabwe

Madagascar

Botswana

Mozambique

Republic of South Africa

are percussion instruments such as shakers and rattles. Musicians use such instruments to play polyrhythms, in which several different rhythms and beats weave around and intertwine with each other. Such rhythms are extremely important, as John E. Kaemmer writes in *The Garland Handbook of African Music*: "This means that drumming [by itself] is considered music, and chanting or speaking words is singing, so long as it is metrical [composed in poetic meter]."[2]

Another important traditional rhythm instrument in southern Africa is the musical bow. These instruments are shaped like hunting bows and have a single string that is held taut by a curved stick. The string is plucked with a thumb and finger, tapped with a stick, or scraped with a stick in the same way a violin is played with a friction bow. Gourds are sometimes attached or held near the musical bow and act as a resonator for the sound. The notes produced by the musical bow can be changed by a player who moves a finger, stick, rock, or bottle up and down the string while plucking it with the other hand.

A more melodic rhythm instrument used in music of southern Africa is the mbira, also known as the thumb piano, finger piano, or *kalimba*. This instrument consists of a soundboard, or resonator, and metal, tonguelike keys that are vibrated when plucked with two thumbs and a forefinger. The soft, xylophone-like music of the mbira is embellished by a continuous, droning buzz that is common to other types of

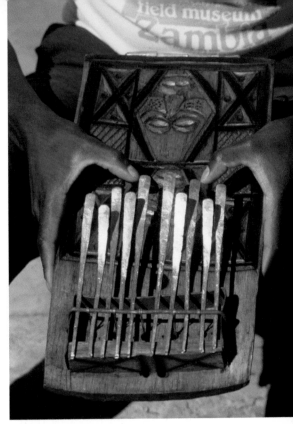

The mbira, or thumb piano, is a popular melodic rhythm instrument.

African music. Paul F. Berliner explains in *The Soul of Mbira*: "This [vibrating] quality is appreciated by African musicians in the same way that Westeners appreciate the sound of the snares on a snare drum or the fuzz-tone on an electric guitar. . . . Once he or she has become accustomed to this quality, the listener or performer would miss it if it were absent; the music would seem naked without it."[3] This sound may be produced by pebbles, small sea shells, or even bottle caps attached to or placed inside the mbira's resonator. Erica Azim provides further details about the instrument on her site Mbira.org:

The mbira . . . consists of 22 to 28 metal keys mounted on a gwariva (hardwood soundboard). . . . Although the metal keys were originally smelted directly from rock containing iron ore, now they may be made from sofa springs, bicycle spokes, car seat springs, and other recycled steel materials. . . . Either metal beads strung on a wire, or bottle tops or shells mounted on a metal plate, are placed on the lower portion of the mbira soundboard to add a buzz which varies from a soft hiss to a tambourine-like sound. Bottle tops or shells are also mounted on the deze [resonator] to increase the buzz. . . . The buzz adds depth and context to the clear tones of the mbira keys, and may be heard as whispering voices, singing, tapping, knocking, wind or rain.[4]

Thomas Mapfumo's Liberation War Music

The mbira has its roots in the traditions of Zimbabwe and has been central to the music of that nation's Shona people for at least one thousand years. In more recent times, music played on the mbira has taken on a political role in the country, which was called Rhodesia after it was colonized by Great Britain in 1890. According to Ronnie Graham in *The Da Capo Guide to Contemporary African Music*, the colonization led to "bitter wars of resistance followed by the steady imposition of white minority rule, neo-apartheid [racial segregation] . . . and a protracted war of national liberation. . . . It would be impossible to ignore this century of division, exploitation and civil war in the analysis of the contemporary musical scene in Zimbabwe."[5]

The leading musician during the quest for liberation in the 1970s was guitarist, singer, and songwriter Thomas Mapfumo, also known as TM or the Lion of Zimbabwe. Born in 1945, Mapfumo began his career playing music from bands the British rulers favored, such as the Beatles and the Rolling Stones. Later, although the dominant white culture looked down on traditional African sounds, calling them primitive and worthless, Mapfumo began to experiment with the mbira, playing the notes of traditional songs on his electric guitar. He also translated the traditional rhythm patterns of the *hosho*, a rattle made from a hollow gourd, for the cymbals of modern drum kits. Mapfumo studied traditional lyrics and proverbs, which he updated or joined with lyrics of protest and revolution that openly called for the violent overthrow of the British government. Mapfumo's new style was called *chimurenga* music, a word that means "liberation war" in the Shona language.

Instead of singing in English, as was common among pop stars in Zimbabwe, Mapfumo sang chimurenga in Shona. In this way he was able to communicate his revolutionary ideas to Zimbabweans in a tongue not understood by the majority of the nation's

The Mbira

The rhythmic and melodic tones of the mbira, or thumb piano, are at the roots of many types of music in southern Africa. On the Web page "The Role of Mbira in Shona Culture", mbira player Erica Azim describes the importance of the instrument to people of Zimbabwe and beyond:

Mbira (the name of both the instrument and the music) is mystical music which has been played for over a thousand years by certain tribes of the Shona people, a group which forms the vast majority of the population of Zimbabwe, and extends into Mozambique. Mbira pervades all aspects of Shona culture, both sacred and secular. Its most important function is as a "telephone to the spirits;" used to contact both deceased ancestors and tribal guardians, at all-night . . . ceremonies [in which] vadzimu (spirits of family ancestors), mhondoro (spirits of deceased chiefs) and makombwe (the most powerful guardian spirits of the Shona) give guidance on family and community matters and exert power over weather and health.

Mbira is required to bring rain during drought, stop rain during floods, and bring clouds when crops are burned by the sun. Mbira is used to chase away harmful spirits, and to cure illnesses. . . . Mbira is included in celebrations of all kinds, including weddings, installation of new chiefs, and, more recently, government events such as independence day and international conferences. . . .

In previous centuries, court musicians played mbira for Shona kings and their diviners. [Today the mbira] is popular throughout Zimbabwe. . . . The Shona mbira is also rapidly becoming known around the world, due to tours by both traditional musicians and Zimbabwean electric bands which include the instrument.

white rulers. In a country where most are illiterate, Mapfumo's lyrics performed the function of newspapers, with words about police actions, martyrs of the independence struggle, and so on. Mapfumo describes the importance of his music in *World Music: The Rough Guide:*

Playing this type of music actually gave us enough moral support to fight the struggle. And to feel that this is my culture and that I am supposed to be someone with a country, someone with a home, someone who is not called a second [class] citizen in his own country. . . . [Before], a lot of our youngsters were playing . . . soul music, [funk], the Beatles, the Rolling Stones. When my music came in, with Shona lyrics, it changed everything.[6]

This change was soon discovered by authorities, who figured out the controversial messages behind Mapfumo's singles such as "Mothers, Send Your Children to War," "Africans Unite," and "Enemy in the Jungle." In 1979 Mapfumo's music was banned from state-controlled radio, and the musician was arrested and held in a prison camp. Authorities could not, however, prevent Mapfumo's chimurenga from being played in dance halls and on revolutionary radio stations. After ninety days of massive protests, Mapfumo was freed.

Zimbabwe was finally liberated from colonial rule in 1980. The new ruler of the land was a repressive black dictator, Robert Mugabe. Mapfumo began singing songs critical of Mugabe and quickly became the target of government harassment. Meanwhile, Mapfumo's music had been discovered by a London-based record company called Earthworks, which released an album

Musician Thomas Mapfumo, shown here at a 2005 performance, inspired the people of Zimbabwe to seek independence.

called *Chimurenga Singles* in Great Britain. The company brought Mapfumo to Europe, where the updated Shona music proved to be an instant hit with concert audiences. After several more critically acclaimed albums, Mapfumo became an international star.

In 2000 Mapfumo heard that the Mugabe regime was planning to assassinate him. Mapfumo fled the country and settled in Eugene, Oregon. Although he misses his home, the Zimbabwean revolutionary continues to play concerts in the United States, Europe, and Africa. Using the hypnotic, trancelike music of mbira, Mapfumo puts forth an almost superhuman effort, playing music from six to nine hours at a time.

South Africa's Complex Musical History

Zimbabwe is but one southern African nation in which a clash of cultures produced a wealth of music forged in protest and resistance. The Republic of South Africa also has a long history of apartheid, colonialism, and government repression of the indigenous population. South Africa is the richest nation on the continent, with a wealth of gold and diamonds that have attracted people from many places including Europe, the United States, and other nations of Africa. This crossroads of wealth and culture has created "the most complex musical history, the greatest profusion of styles and the most intensely developed recording industry anywhere in Africa,"[7] according to *World Music: The Rough Guide.*

American jazz musician Duke Ellington, pictured here with his band, influenced South African music.

The roots of this musical cornucopia can be traced to professional African American musicians who first visited South Africa in the late nineteenth century after gold was discovered in Johannesburg. At that time, both white and black South Africans were entertained by black American vocal groups, ragtime piano players, and gospel singers from the American South. By the 1920s, the American jazz music of Duke Ellington, Louis Armstrong, and others played a role in the development of South African dance music. Local bands, such as the Jazz Maniacs, incorporated elements of American jazz and swing with *marabi,* a style of music from Johannesburg's huge slums.

Marabi consists of a repetitive melody and three chords played repeatedly on the piano. This music, played by impoverished African musicians, was accompanied by whatever battered instruments could be found. These included traditional shakers that consisted of cans filled with pebbles. Guitars, banjos, and small accordions called concertinas were also used to play marabi. In this free-form style of music, singers or musicians might incorporate snatches of melodies from popular songs, hymns, or traditional African songs.

"The Lion Sleeps Tonight"

While marabi music remained popular, another style of music evolved in the province of Natal. This style, known by the tongue-twisting name *isicathamiya*, would later introduce South African music to the world. Isicathamiya was vocal music sung a cappella, or without instrumental backing. The genre was developed by Zulu men who were forced to leave their native villages and labor in gold mines and factories. Separated from their wives and families, the men passed the time on Sundays, their only day off work, by participating in music and dance competitions that were judged by complex rules.

One of the most celebrated winners of the isicathamiya contests was Solomon Linda and his band the Original Evening Birds. Linda wrote the song "Mbube," or "The Lion," and recorded it in 1939. The song was the first South African record to sell 100,000 copies. After this success, dozens of vocal groups with as many as fifteen members were formed

to imitate Linda's style, which included the use of a tenor, or high lead vocalist singing above group harmonies in every range including at least three men singing deep bass harmony. Dressed in flashy uniforms, the singing band members executed dance steps known as "tip toes" because they were choreographed so as to not disturb the camp security guards. As a tribute to the song that inspired so many musicians, the vocal style itself acquired a new name, *mbube*, "the lion." In *Goodtime Kings: Emerging African Pop*, Billy Bergman describes the musical aspects of the style:

> The voices in mbube make lush, uniform choral harmonies, all singing together in short phrases. Then they may break up into rhythm and melody sections or overlapping call-and-response, with a prominent deep bass voice. The sound may be organized without chord progressions, or it may verge on a gospel style. A few groups even have lyrics on Christianity, while others discuss rural problems.[8]

The original song "Mbube" eventually became one of the first songs that would come to be called world music. With the title changed to "Wimoweh," the song was a huge hit in the United States and Europe in 1950 for the folk group the Weavers. In 1961 the song was slightly rewritten by the Tokens and became a hit again, this time with the title "The Lion Sleeps Tonight." In 1994 "Wimoweh/The Lion Sleeps

Johnny Clegg and Savuka

Although native Africans dominate the South African world music scene, not all musicians from that nation are black. In fact, one of the best-selling world musicians from South Africa is Johnny Clegg, a white guitarist, singer, and songwriter born in England. Clegg's career is described on the "Afropop Worldwide" Web site:

When Johnny Clegg first brought his half-Zulu, half-white band Juluka to Europe [in 1981], amazed audiences saw a young white man singing in Zulu, playing traditional guitar riffs and nailing difficult, high-kicking Indlamu war dances with his lithe partner Dudu Zulu. French fans dubbed Clegg "Le Zoulou Blanc" (The White Zulu). Born in England, raised in Zimbabwe and Zambia, Clegg landed in Johannesburg, South Africa, a shy, inarticulate boy of 12. . . . A chance encounter with an old Zulu street guitarist caught Clegg's ear, and led him to Zulu culture. Clegg teamed up with guitarist and songwriter Sipho Mchunu to form Juluka. In South Africa, Juluka alarmed authorities by presenting black and white musicians together on stage. When the group's potent marriage of Zulu war songs and English folk-rock caught on, Juluka faced bomb threats, concert shutdowns and racism from both the black and white music industries. Mchunu retired to his farm in 1986, and Clegg formed a more western pop-oriented outfit called Savuka, which continues to record hits and wow audiences, especially abroad. Savuka performed its resonant tribute to political victims of apartheid, "Asimbonanga," at Nelson Mandela's inauguration.

Johnny Clegg wows the crowd in a 2003 performance.

Tonight" was embraced by a new generation when it was used in the Disney animated film *The Lion King.*

Groaners and Homegrown Vocals

Even as their music was selling in the United States and Europe, life was changing for the worse for blacks in South Africa. In 1948 the National Party government came to power and began enforcing a strict regime of apartheid. New laws prevented black and white musicians from playing together and from playing to multiracial audiences.

The government bulldozed popular black urban neighborhoods that were centers of South African music and forced residents to relocate to distant new neighborhoods called townships.

Though forced to live under extremely repressive conditions, South African musicians continued to innovate. Mbube music was adopted by female vocalists who sang soaring five-part harmonies. The women often performed with a gravelly voiced male vocalist, known as a "groaner," who would keep up a running rap-like commentary with the singers and make

The Mahotella Queens were part of the most popular mbaqanga, or "homegrown" group, in South Africa during the 1960s.

comments about news, gossip, or people in the audience. His raspy, deep voice acted as a counterpoint to the women's high-spirited harmonies.

This rhythmic, danceable pop music style came to be known as mbaqanga, a Zulu word that translates to "homegrown." By the early 1960s, the most popular mbaqanga group in South Africa was Simon Mahlatini and the Mahotella Queens. Mahlatini was the foremost groaner, and concerts with the Queens were attended by tens of thousands of people.

Although protest music was forbidden by the South African government, mbaqanga singers often incorporated political slogans into their lyrics. The song "Azikwelwa," or "We Refuse to Ride," was about a bus boycott and was sung at protests. Mbaqanga lyrics also incorporated chants such as "Free Mandela"—a reference to antiapartheid leader Nelson Mandela, who was imprisoned for decades because of his political activities.

The Road to *Graceland*

With its repetitive chords, traditional African melodies, and call-and-response style, mbaqanga also formed the basis for South African jazz. One of South Africa's most talented jazz musicians, trumpeter Hugh Masekela, was raised on marabi music and in the 1950s played to audiences at concert variety shows called Township Jazz put together by white promoters.

One of the most popular female vocalists of the jazz era was Miriam Makeba. After recording with her all-female band the Skylarks in the mid-1950s, Makeba played the female lead in a 1959 Broadway-style musical *King Kong*, about a South African boxing champ. Masekela was in the orchestra of this production, known as a jazz opera, and he and Makeba soon became international stars after *King Kong* had a successful one-year run in London. In 1967 Masekela briefly became an international pop star with the hit "Grazin' in the Grass." Makeba, however, became an exile after she testified about the horrors of apartheid before a United Nations commission in 1963. The government of South Africa revoked her citizenship, and Makeba moved to the United States.

Except for Makeba and Masekela, few South African musicians made inroads into the international record markets of the 1960s and 1970s. Most Americans never heard the music until they were exposed to it from an unlikely source, Paul Simon, who in earlier years had a string of number-one hits with the group Simon and Garfunkel. In 1986 Simon released the album *Graceland*, which featured the isicathamiya singing of Ladysmith Black Mambazo, a group that had been popular in South Africa since the release of their first album, *Amabutho*, in 1973. (Ladysmith is the hometown of group leader Joseph Shabalala, and Black Mambazo means "Black Axe," referring to the group's powerful vocals that would "chop down" all challengers in isicathamiya contests.)

The critically acclaimed *Graceland* went on to become the best-selling album of the 1980s, and eventually sold 14 million copies. In addition to winning several Grammy Awards, the album brought world music to a large, new audience for the first time. In 1987 Simon released the video *Graceland: The African Concert*, featuring Ladysmith Black Mambazo, Miriam Makeba, Hugh Masekela, and a backup band of talented South African musicians.

In 1988 Simon produced *Shaka Zulu* by Ladysmith Black Mambazo, which initially sold more than one hundred thousand copies and won a Grammy in a new category, world music. Today, the thirty albums produced by Lady-Smith Black Mambazo are among the most recognized sounds of South Africa and world music in general.

A New Generation

While many of South Africa's most renowned world music performers have been playing for decades, a new generation of performers has emerged that combine Western pop music sensibilities with unique African styles. This highly produced music, known as "bubblegum" by both its fans and detractors, features electronic keyboards,

Music of Madagascar

The island of Madagascar, off the coast of southeastern Africa, is known for its unusual natural beauty. One and a half times the size of California, the nation also has a rich musical tradition influenced by the island's eighteen indigenous tribes, as well as outsiders from Europe, South America, and elsewhere. One of its most exceptional bands, Tarika, is fronted by two sisters, Hanitra Rasoanaivo and Noro Raharimalala. Hanitra composes songs with messages about Madagascar's often-troubled political, social, and environmental history.

Tarika performs their music on modern instruments but also uses traditional ones such as the *valiha*, a long, tubular bamboo zither with between sixteen and twenty-one strings that produces a sound of almost unearthly beauty. The *kabosy,* similar to a guitar but with a box-shaped body and four to eight strings, is used as a rhythm instrument.

The blend of vocal harmonies and modern and traditional instruments have made Tarika one of the most popular bands on the world music scene.

synthesizers, and computerized drum machines playing a modified disco beat. Brenda Fassi is among the leading stars of bubblegum, and her songs and fashion sense have been favorably compared to those of Madonna. While bubblegum has become the dominant sound in South Africa, singer Lucky Dube has achieved stardom singing Jamaican-style reggae. Dube began his career singing Zulu mbaqanga in the 1970s but switched to reggae after hearing Jamaican reggae superstar Bob Marley's 1980 concert in Zimbabwe. By the 1990s, Dube's unique African reggae albums were typically selling five hundred thousand copies each, and the singer was one of South Africa's most popular recording stars. Today he is known as the reggae king of South Africa.

Like that of Mapfumo and thousands of other talented musicians from southern Africa, Dube's music was created under conditions of harsh racism and subjugation that served to destroy the spirits of many others. However, because these artists channeled their energies into musical expression, the world music from southern Africa has brought joy to millions of listeners around the globe.

Chapter Two

Music of West and Central Africa

The broad swath of land that makes up western and central Africa is home to a remarkable array of influential musicians. From Senegal, Guinea, and Ghana on West Africa's Atlantic shores to the inland nations of Mali, Nigeria, Cameroon, and the Democratic Republic of Congo, there exists a musical tradition in which much of the world's music is rooted.

Most of the well-known musicians from West and Central Africa have connections to two major European cities, London and Paris. This is a result of history. Gambia, Sierra Leone, Ghana, and Nigeria share a British colonial background. Senegal, Mali, Guinea, Niger, and others were part of France's former empire. The United States also has ties to Africa. Beginning in the seventeenth century, the majority of black slaves brought to North America were from West Africa. The ancient African musical influences of the slaves are at the cen- ter of musical styles such as blues, ragtime, jazz, rock and roll, and even hip-hop. Today, the influences have come full circle with American popu- lar music and instruments such as electric and bass guitars, synthesizers, pianos, and drum kits having their own impact on African world music, sometimes called Afropop. Central to these complex rhythms, melodies, and styles are musical traditions that are hundreds of years old.

The Musical Storytellers

The roots of modern African world mu- sic can be traced back to an ancient caste of musician known as *Jelis, Griots*, or *Grios* (pronounced GREE-ohs). These storytelling musicians, part of Mali's an- cient Mande or Mandingo culture, first emerged in the twelfth century, when they were known for singing flattering songs of praise about nobles and other patrons who employed them. Griot mu- sician Foday Musa Suso from Mali de- scribes his profession:

A griot is an oral historian. Griots were trusted court advisors to the kings of West Africa from the 12th century to the 20th. Every griot wanted . . . to recite the history of the kingdom, and to pass it down from father to son. History wasn't written down—everything was memorized and recited or sung. . . . Griots are travelling families. You cannot be a griot and stay in one place. Even today, you see griots travelling . . . moving between cities and towns. The griots are walking libraries, with knowledge of the past, present and future of our people. . . . Some of our songs last two days. . . . Telling [eight] hundred years of history takes a long time.[9]

In the Middle Ages, griots accompanied themselves on wooden xylophones called *balafons* and various types of drums such as the *doundoun, djembe*, and *tama*, or talking drum. The most revered instrument, however, was a seven-stringed instrument called a *simbi*, a cross between a harp and a lute. Over the centuries, this instrument grew and evolved into the *kora*, or *cora*, a twenty-one stringed instrument that is widely used today in the world music emanating from West Africa.

The kora, with a harplike sound reminiscent of a babbling brook or gentle rainstorm, is played by musicians from Gambia, Mali, Guinea, and Senegal. The body of the instrument is made from a calabash gourd cut in half and covered in cow skin. The strings are plucked with both hands using the forefingers and thumbs.

In Europe, griot Mory Kanté has sold more than 1 million albums featuring his fast-paced, electrified kora playing. Bergman describes a Kanté performance: "Mory came out of a puff

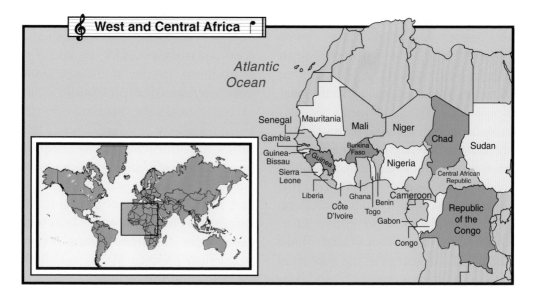

West and Central Africa

Atlantic Ocean

Senegal Mauritania Mali Niger
Gambia
Guinea-Bissau Burkina Faso Chad Sudan
Sierra Leone Guinea Nigeria
Central African Republic
Liberia Ghana Benin Cameroon
Côte D'Ivoire Togo
Gabon Republic of the Congo
Congo

of smoke, wearing a shimmering pink suit, playing an electric kora, and backed by a full electric ensemble. He drove the entire audience onto the dancefloor."[10]

In the 1980s, Kanté moved to Paris, where his 1986 song. "Yeke Yeke" sold over a million copies and was a major hit in European dance halls. A remix of this modernized Guinea love song was later used in 2000 for the soundtrack of the Leonardo De Caprio film *The Beach.* In 2005 Kanté continued to take electrified griot music to European audiences, touring Belgium, Italy, Greece, Great Britain, and other nations.

Musician Vieux Diop plays the kora, *a twenty-one string instrument.*

Youssou N'Dour: The Star of Dakar

The griot tradition is not unique to Mali. In Senegal, singers of praise are known as *gewel* or *gawlo*. In the past two decades, there has been a musical breakthrough in Senegal by musicians who have melded the ancient *gewel* tradition with modern musical styles. Those who have done so, according to Mark Hudson in *World Music Volume 1: Africa, Europe and the Middle East*, have had an impact on world music "out of all proportion to the country's population."[11]

Whereas Mali's music is kora-based, Senegalese music has been strongly influenced by Latin American dance music such as rumba and mambo. First introduced in the Senegal capital of Dakar by the nation's colonial rulers in the 1960s, the Latin sound was Africanized over the years. The Spanish lyrics were converted to Wolof, the native language of Senegal, and were sung in a high-pitched style. Traditional Wolof drum rhythms were introduced along with the *tama* and *saba*, an upright drum similar to a conga.

In 1977 a group of Dakar's most talented musicians formed a group called Étoile de Dakar (Star of Dakar) that mixed griot singing with bright, jazzy, Latin-style horns. The band further Africanized the music by adding a drum-heavy rhythm section based on polyrhythmic interplay between the various drummers. Playing this new style of music, called *mbalax*, the Wolof word for percussion-based music, the band was an instant success in Dakar. Although their music was original, part of their appeal was the band's attitude, as Hudson writes: "They were young and defiantly proud of their Senegalese identity. They sang almost entirely in Wolof, flaunting the tradi-

Mali Guitarists

The Mande music from Mali and Guinea is extremely popular in the West, particularly in Europe. Electric guitarists play an important role in the music, as Eric Charry writes on the "West African Music" Web page:

Mande guitarists are active players in an unbroken and still-vibrant tradition that goes back to the thirteenth-century founding of the Mande, or Mali, Empire. That tradition is primarily guarded by jelis, hereditary professional verbal/musical artisans. The acoustic guitar was first picked up in the 1920s or 1930s by jelis who began an Africanization process by adapting their balafon (xylophone), nkoni (lute), and kora (harp) repertoires and playing styles to it. The rise of modern Mande music and of the electric guitar began with the independence of Guinea in 1958 when the new government launched a sweeping modernization policy in which European musical instruments (including electric guitars) were handed out, musicians were made civil servants, and a network of regional and national orchestras was established. Mali soon followed suit. Jelis used the electric guitar as the main vehicle for transferring their local repertories to these new urban electric groups.

tional griot origins of their music and their own images as [just regular] lads on the corner."[12]

The band's handsome lead singer, Youssou N'Dour, born in 1959, led the band with unique "scat" vocals. Scat singing consists of improvised strings of nonsensical syllables with vocal growls and rumbles meant to sound like a deeply soulful trumpet solo. N'Dour also added other vocal techniques, according to Tom Schnabel in *Rhythm Planet: The Great World Music Makers*. These included "*bakou-trilling* (a traditional chant), and *tasso* (a kind of rap) to create a full and very rhythmic sound—dance music at its best."[13] N'Dour wrote lyrics in the griot tradition. According to Hudson:

He sang about the people's joys: their traditional festivals, the excitement of the city, the importance of respecting one's parents and remembering one's roots. Above all, he sang for women: he used words and phrases traditionally associated with women, praised rich and famous women, praised his own mother, and, by implication, all mothers and all women.[14]

Étoile de Dakar was performing at a time when Dakar was growing into a large city with a burgeoning youth culture. In this milieu, N'Dour soon became Senegal's first pop star. Within a few years, N'Dour changed the name of his band to Super Étoile de Dakar and took over complete control of the band's music and business affairs. By 1983 N'Dour's success allowed him to open Thiosanne, his own nightclub in Dakar, where he performed nearly every night. The singer's contribution to world music might have ended there were it not for a gig in a small London nightclub in 1984, when pop superstar Peter Gabriel happened to be in the audience. As Gabriel later stated, N'Dour's voice "sent shivers down my spine."[15] The British star befriended the singer and hired him to sing on his 1986 album *So*. Gabriel later booked Super Étoile de Dakar to open for him on his world tour that year. Paul Simon heard of N'Dour and invited him to play drums on *Graceland*.

The next year, N'Dour's first solo recording, *The Lion*, was released on Virgin Records. The album contained

Youssou N'Dour was Senegal's first pop star. He is pictured here performing in France in 2002.

Female *Jelis*

Men dominate the music scene in most West African nations. However, in Mali, female griots, called jelis *or* jelimusolu, *are among the most popular stars, as Lucy Duran writes in* World Music Volume 1: Africa, Europe and the Middle East:

[T]he] famed women jelis' . . . status as local superstars, who take the lion's share of fees and command adoring audiences, is unique in West Africa. . . . Their flamboyant personalities and independent life-styles have made them the subjects of intense, often malicious, gossip. "It's brought us many problems from jealousy and intolerance," says singer Ami Koita, "but personally I have had no choice but to go ahead anyway; this is my destiny."

One of the first women singers to become popular after independence [in 1960] was Fanta Sacko from Kita. She called her style jamana kura (new age), delivering light, rhythmic and melodious love songs, accompanied on two acoustic guitars in non-standard tunings . . . imitating the kora and the insect-like sound of the ngoni [plucked lute]. Referred to . . . as bajourou, this represents the most popular trend of guitar-based music in Guinea and Mali since the 1970s. Her most famous song, "Jarabi," has been recorded in dozens of cover versions by most of Mali's best-known artists. Apart from being a beautiful minor-key tune, "Jarabi" was a local hit because of its lyrics, which advocate passionate love above all other feelings.

songs about social and environmental problems such as toxic waste pollution, economic displacement, the oppression of women, corrupt politicians, disease, poverty, hunger, and other issues affecting Senegal and other African nations. The albums that followed made N'Dour one of the top recording artists in the world music genre. Over the years, he has dedicated his time to raising awareness of political issues by playing concerts such as the Amnesty International Human Rights Now! tour with Bruce Springsteen and Sting. Never one to forget his musical roots, N'Dour built a recording studio in Dakar to release several cassettes a year for the home market in Senegal, where CDs remain an expensive luxury. He also started a music label to promote other Senegalese artists who sing about local concerns. While many other world music artists relocated to London, Paris, or the United States after finding success, N'Dour has remained in Senegal, where he works with local musicians and producers to create modern griot music for fans across the globe.

Nigeria's Juju Music

The griot legacy and Latin beat that inspired N'Dour has also been influential in other West African nations. In Nigeria, Latin music was first introduced to the indigenous Yoruba population by Brazilian and Cuban merchants in the nineteenth century. By the 1920s, the Yoruba, who had a long tradition of singing songs of praise, criticism, and morality, had transformed Brazilian dance music, called samba, into a unique African sound. Backed by banjos, guitars, drums, and shakers, singers rewrote traditional Yoruba proverbs to describe urban problems in the Nigerian city of Lagos. This homegrown style, known as palm-wine music, was very popular among workers such as truck drivers, carpenters, and sailors.

In the 1930s, one of the most popular palm-wine singers, "Babe" Tunde King, began calling the music juju, possibly after the "ju ju" sound made by a small hexagonal tambourine of Brazilian heritage that was used in the music. The British record label His Master's Voice saw commercial potential in the music and before long, juju records were being sold by the thousands in Lagos.

In 1957 juju was modernized by I.K. Dairo who, with his band the Blue Spots, added electric guitars and amplifiers to the music. The amplification allowed players to bring in louder, traditional percussion, and the talking drum was also added to the mix. While early juju bands usually had no more than three musicians, the Blue Spots grew to ten musicians.

In the 1970s, juju developed rapidly, thanks to King Sunny Ade, a member of the royal family in Oshogbo, Nigeria, and the leading star of the style. As the Nigerian public watched with fascination, the visionary Ade added as many players as possible to his band. Before long, King Sunny Ade and his African Beats boasted twenty to thirty musicians playing trap drums; several keyboards and synthesizers; nearly a dozen traditional drums, talking drums, and shakers; four guitar players; female backing vocalists; and the Hawaiian pedal steel guitar most often found in American country music. This allowed Ade to leave behind the old-style juju songs of three minutes and create long, drawn-out musical jams that lasted up to twenty minutes.

In 1977 Ade was billed as the King of Juju Music and was a rising star on the international music scene. François Bensignor describes Ade's key to success: "His guitar line-up, weaving intricate melodic patterns against a backdrop of thundering percussion, the call-and-response "conversations" of the talking drums, and the infectiously winning, "African-prince" style of the man himself—all gave off strong commercial signals."[16]

In 1982 Ade was signed by London-based Island Records and billed as the African Bob Marley. His first album for Island, *Juju Music*, was recorded in 1982 and sold two hundred thousand copies, an impressive number for an African act. Although his subsequent records did not sell as well in the United States and Europe, Ade remained popular in Africa, where he continued to play and record. In 1998 Ade staged a comeback in the West with *Odu*, a collection of traditional Yoruba songs that was nominated for a Grammy Award for best world music album. In 2004, Ade released his 112th album, *Divine Shield*, and launched a world tour. The following year, his appearances in clubs in the United States and Canada drew large, appreciative crowds, and his fans continued to call him the King of Juju.

King Sunny Ade is the leading star of juju music.

Soukous: The Preeminent African Sound

The Latin influence behind traditional juju is also found in the Democratic Republic of Congo, where soukous, named after a popular 1960s dance, has evolved since the 1930s. Soukous is also known as the rumba of the Congo, and the rumba beat from Cuba has played a central role in the development of the style. In the roundabout sphere of influence typical of many world music styles, the rumba beat itself evolved in the eighteenth century as a result of African slaves in the Caribbean mixing their traditional sounds with the music of their Spanish overseers. When the rumba returned to Africa, the infectious beat was blended with indigenous music made by Congo villagers. In this way, soukous traveled to Cuba, was transformed by Afro-Caribbean culture, and journeyed back to Africa, where it was used to create an entirely new sound. Today soukous, with its lyrics sung in French and indigenous Lingala, is among the most popular in the world music genre. Susan Orlean described the sound in a 2002 article in the *New Yorker*:

[What] made soukous the preeminent music in Africa was its sound, the voluptuous interplay of

Pygmy Fusion

African world music is not limited to sounds emerging from large cities in Senegal, Nigeria, and the Congo. Deep within the rain forests of the Central African nation of Cameroon, traditional music made by the Baka people, known as Pygmies because of their small stature, has made surprising inroads in the West.

The Baka people of Cameroon are known for melodious, rhythmic songs.

The indigenous hunter-gatherers sing polyphonic songs, that is, music with two or more independent melodic parts sounded together. These choruses are sung all day, as people bathe, cook, and perform other activities. Some of the melodious, rhythmic songs are used by hunters to enthrall animals so that they are easier to hunt with spears and nets.

The hypnotic music created by the Baka has long been of interest to Westerners. In the 1950s, Pygmy music was released on records available in the United States and Europe. In 1993, however, Pygmy polyphony exploded into the world music market with the release of the *Deep Forest* CD. This album, produced by two French pop stars, Eric Mouquet and Michael Sanchez, fused digital keyboards and percussion with field recordings of Baka singers. *Deep Forest* sold over 2.5 million copies in three years and remains the best-selling world music fusion album of all time. The Pygmies whose magical singing contributed to the record's success received few royalties for their songs, however.

Today, the Pygmy lifestyle in Cameroon is threatened. Hunters have complained that their songs no longer work on the animals because of the noise created by logging and encroaching civilization. Some are hoping that new Pygmy fusion albums will be made available in the West with the royalties going to preserve the forest and save the homeland of the Baka singers.

three or four or even five guitars, swirling around keening melodies and a dreamy, compelling beat. It is emotional, complex music, with the brightness and propulsion and hot guitars of popular music but with a less hurried, mounting intensity. It sounds neither contemporary nor old; it is melodic and highly structured, even orchestral, but also powerfully rhythmic and cyclic, like a chant. You can dance for hours and hours to soukous music; it has that kind of drive. But it is also strangely, ineffably poignant. Even the biggest, brassiest soukous songs have a wistful undercurrent, the sound of something longed for or lost.[17]

The commercial potential of soukous was first recognized by Greek immigrants who opened recording studios in the Congo capital of Kinshasa in the early 1950s. This initiated what was called the belle epoque, or "beautiful era," of Congolese rumba. In the mid-fifties, guitarist Luambo Makiadi, known as Franco, gathered a dozen of Kinshasa's finest studio musicians to form the Orchestra Kinois Jazz, or OK Jazz band. Franco's dazzling guitar abilities were matched only by his prolific songwriting talents. Known as the grand master of rumba and the godfather of

African music, Franco wrote more than one thousand songs and recorded 150 albums before his death in 1989.

During the forty years that spanned Franco's career, soukous became the sound of Congo, heard everywhere on city streets blasting from homes, businesses, clubs, and cars. But in the 1970s, the repressive political climate of the nation drove many soukous producers and musicians out of the Congo. The music was reborn in Paris, where more than 1 million French-speaking Africans moved over the years. By 1980 all the biggest soukous stars, including Franco, Tabu Ley Rochereau, and Joseph Kabasele, were regularly playing in Paris nightclubs that catered to the African community. New on this scene was Kanda Bongo Man, who created a fast-paced party style of soukous that was an instant hit with the Parisian club crowd.

With its best musicians based in France, the sounds of soukous once again traveled across continents to inspire new cultures. Like juju and other sounds of Africa, the music has transcended borders, political repression, and the vagaries of the commercial market. With its infectious dance beat, socially conscious lyrics, and stunning instrumentation, Afropop is sure to remain a force in world music for decades to come.

Chapter Three

Music of North Africa and the Middle East

People in northern Africa have musical traditions dating back more than five thousand years. As long ago as 3000 B.C., musicians in Egypt played instruments that were the ancestors to modern flutes, oboes, trumpets, kettle drums, harps, lyres, guitars, lutes, and even pipe organs. Beginning in about the tenth century, Middle Eastern traders carried these instruments to Europe, where they were adapted to fit local tastes and talents.

Ancient instruments are but one part of the North African musical tradition. In Arab societies, poetry is considered to be the highest art form. In this milieu, lyrics are often based on classic poems and the words are as important as the music. As Simon Broughton writes in *World Music: The Rough Guide:*

[North African] singers and writers, through the language and emotional power of popular song, have been influential in determining the identity of nations, expressing the hopes of their people, and occasionally threatening the states themselves. Music has thus retained its unique power in the Arab world.[18]

Even as singers have long played a vital role in Arab classical music, they have also been central to introducing their music to the world stage. Like traditions from other parts of Africa, modern Arab music combines old and new genres, melding centuries-old structures and instrumentation with Western funk, rhythm and blues, jazz, soul, and even hip-hop and electronic dance styles. This synthesis of genres has made North African music more accessible to Western ears and has occasionally propelled it to the top of the world music charts.

Like western, southern, and central African musicians, many top artists from northern Africa have been forced to leave their native lands. Repressive governments ban musicians who sing about social and political problems; some are even jailed and killed. This means that northern African world music stars are more often seen and heard in Great Britain, France, Canada, and the United States than in their homelands. A positive effect has resulted from this unfortunate situation, however, as new audiences and new opportunities have opened for those performing in Europe and North America.

"Women of the Cold Shoulder"

Perhaps nothing better exemplifies the clash between repressive officials and modern Arab music than the defiant urban pop music called *rai,* a style developed in Oran, Algeria, starting in the 1970s. Rai singers, who have been compared with American rappers, improvise lyrics about street life and survival in a society in which Islamic fundamentalists forbid people to sing about romance, women, or alcohol.

Music historians trace the roots of rap to the African griot tradition, and the inspiration for rai also comes from ancient culture. Rai has similarities to the oral traditions of the local Bedouins and Berbers, two of Algeria's indigenous cultures. Unlike rap, however, rai can trace its origins to women, specifically those who attended weddings, in which they were segregated from men. According to the singer Khaled, known as the King of Rai, "The women would gather together, singing, talking, and saying things about the men that they couldn't say otherwise in mixed company. *Ya rai* means something akin to 'tell it like it is.'"[19]

This controversial music was performed only in private until the 1930s, when young women from the lowest ranks of society took rai to steamy bars, hashish dens, cafés, and bordellos of the coastal city of Oran, called the "little Paris" of Algeria. These Muslim women, or *cheikhas*, were peasants, orphans, and laborers who lived in a world of poverty and hopelessness.

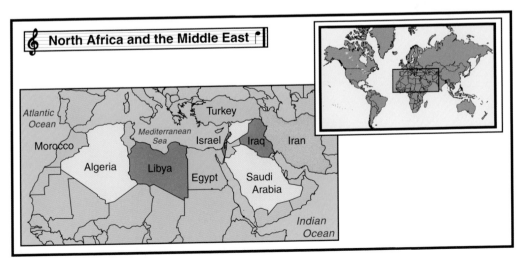

North Africa and the Middle East

Atlantic Ocean

Morocco

Algeria

Mediterranean Sea

Turkey

Israel

Libya

Egypt

Iraq

Iran

Saudi Arabia

Indian Ocean

Also known as "women of the cold shoulder"[20] because they were shunned by polite society, the cheikhas adapted the ancient chanting style of Bedouin poets to speak to modern concerns such as colonialism, violence, crime, arranged marriages, overcrowding, prostitution, and other social issues. Singing in Oran street slang and broken French, the women added bawdy sexual rhymes and humorous observations of street life that shocked traditionalists. All were sung over the highly percussive beat of drums and flutes played by men.

Rai music was abhorrent to the nation's religious leaders, so singers were forced to hide their identities. Cheikhas covered their faces with veils, used amusing nicknames, and never allowed their pictures to be printed on record or cassette covers. When performing, they traveled from town to town with the male musicians and a man who acted as a master of ceremonies. His job was to introduce the singers, shout out dedications to the men in the audience, and badger audience members for money.

Khaled: The King of *Rai*

By the late 1960s, the rai movement had grown to include both women and men singers. The terms *cheb* and *chebba*—young man and young woman—were used to describe the singers, who sometimes mixed rai with Western styles such as jazz and rumba. Lyrics

The singer Khaled (right) is known as the King of Rai, *a type of urban pop music developed in Algeria.*

remained controversial, as the singers often made a point of mocking public officials. Meanwhile, Western records by the Beatles, the Rolling Stones, and soul artists James Brown and Otis Redding had made their way to Northern Africa, inspiring a new generation of rai artists. Two young musicians, trumpeter Bellemou Messaoud and singer Belkacem Bouteldja, updated the traditional sound of rai, using saxophones, trumpets, and accordions instead of flutes. The traditional metallic-sounding *guellal* drum was replaced by the much louder Indian tabla, which had a richer sound. Other musical styles, such as Moroccan and Egyptian pop music, Spanish flamenco, soul, reggae, and rock were added to the new sound, which came to be called pop rai. This happened at a time when inexpensive cassette players were first available in Algeria, which allowed young people to buy inexpensive cassette recording equipment to mass produce original music.

One such producer was a young cheb known by the name of Khaled. Influenced by renowned Egyptian singer Umm Kulthum, the French chanteuse Edith Piaf, and the American rocker Elvis Presley, Khaled learned to play bass, guitar, and harmonica as a child in Oran. As a young artist, Khaled risked his life producing cassettes that contained antifundamentalist lyrics, paeans to human rights, and views on other controversial subjects such as the pleasures of drinking and romance. By the 1980s, Khaled was one of Algeria's top rai singers, and his songs combined funk dance grooves with hypnotic trance rhythms. His lyrics, however— such as "Hey, Mama, your daughter wants me"[21] in the song "So That Is What You Desire"—earned the ire of Islamic conservatives. Explaining the controversy, Khaled states: "In Algeria . . . it is forbidden to sing about women. In all the classical songs, women are usually represented by gazelles or other metaphors. I go further and sing about real love between a man and a woman."[22]

Such sentiments enraged Islamic terrorists and led to countless death threats against Khaled, who does not take such threats lightly. Terrorists have murdered several rai artists, including singer Cheb Hansi and producer Rachid Baba-Ahmed, who revolutionized the music in the 1980s by adding synthesizers and drum machines.

Top Ten in France

Worried about his safety and desiring to express himself without restraint, Khaled immigrated to France, a move that led to world music stardom in the early 1990s. Working with Parisian and American producers, Khaled developed an international sound that combined digital instruments with traditional melodies and topical lyrics. In 1992 his single "Didi" was the first song sung in Arabic to reach the top ten on the French charts. Khaled added new influences in 1996, when he traveled to Jamaica to record songs with veteran reggae session musicians.

The Grandmother of *Rai*

In 1936 Cheikha Remitti became a national sensation in Algeria by singing about topics considered controversial by powerful religious leaders. Born in 1923, this mother of ten has provided an inspiration for rai *music, a style sometimes referred to as Algerian rap. Remitti's story is told by Andy Morgan in* World Music, Volume 1:

Cheikha Remitti, the grandmother of Algerian rai music . . . is the greatest of all the cheikhas, the women singers of western Algeria who sing and improvise their raunchy lyrical snapshots of daily low-life in a thick, highly flavored dialect unique to the country around the great seaport of Oran. Her notoriety is founded on her remarkable skill with words, her acute improvisational abilities and her fearlessness. Only those ears tuned in to the cheeky and comical patois . . . can appreciate her razor sharp talent for satirical improvisation. Inspiration comes to her at night and, in her words, "like a swarm of bees attacking my head." She sings about the pleasures of booze ("Some people adore God. I adore beer."), the repugnant attitude of old men towards their young brides . . . the pleasures of sex . . . about cars, telephones . . . and the homesick agonies of the emigrant.

All this verbal wizardry is belted out in a voice that could grate the hide off a rhinoceros, a deep soulful rasp that pulsates to the raw rhythmic trance of the metallic guellal drums and interweaves with the swirling barren wail of the *gasba* (a rosewood desert flute). On stage, Remitti flirts outrageously with her audience, distilling all the sexual power of an Elvis groin thrust into the rhythmic hike of her eyebrows and the flutter of her shimmying shoulders, the glint of her gold teeth vying with the wicked sparkle in her eyes.

Describing his popularity, Khaled comments: "In France or the U.S., people who don't understand a word of what you're singing still get into the groove and love it. . . . There is something in the blood, a feeling you get through music that doesn't really have to be understood by the lyrics."[23]

Khaled has inspired a new generation of rai artists to experiment with a variety of musical styles. In 1998 he headlined the first all-Algerian lineup at a large stadium in France with up-coming stars Cheb Mami and rai singer (as well as young prince) Faudel. Another performer that night was Rachid Taha, a French-born Algerian who combines punk rock with Arabic music. In 2005 the King of Rai embarked on a successful tour of the United States. Khaled continues to sing to his fans in countries on three continents.

Egyptian Street Music

Khaled's popularity extends beyond Algeria and the Arab world. The style Khaled pioneered also has its counterpart in Egypt, where *shaabi* singers express the viewpoints common to working-class people who live in poverty in Cairo, one of the most densely populated cities on Earth.

Shaabi, which means "of the people," got its start in the early 1970s when young people began combining an ancient storytelling tradition called *mawal* with Western and electric instruments. According to David Lodge and Bill Badley in *World Music, mawal* is "a freely improvised vocal in which the singer impresses upon the listener the depth of his or her sorrowful complaint."[24] With shaabi, however, singers melded their "sorrowful complaints" with fast-paced, danceable rhythms and repetitive, catchy choruses. The lyrical content is similar to rai, as Banning Eyre explains on the Afropop World-wide Web site:

Shamelessly rude and comic in its themes and lyrics . . . [the]

music can evoke sadness and nostalgia, but more often fits tales of survival in the city and working class pride to breathless rhythms and rough-edged musical productions. [Shaabi singers] shocked some listeners and delighted others with unabashed straight talk and new takes on traditional social music. In shaabi, old, folkloric chants slide into rap, while hand-clapping and dancing oud [Middle Eastern lute] melodies ornament slamming, bass-driven dance mixes.[25]

Egyptian shaabi *singer Hakim performs in Lebanon.*

The Captain of Nubian Music

The Nubian people resided in southern Egypt for thousands of years, before their homeland was destroyed to build the Aswan High Dam on the Nile River in the 1960s. While the Nubians scattered to communities in Sudan and Cairo, their ancient style of music was kept alive by Ali Hassan Kuban, who melded it with jazz and other modern sounds. Banning Eyre describes the music and the man on the "Afropop Worldwide" Web site.

Once dubbed the "Captain of Nubian Music," and later the "Godfather" of the genre, Ali Hassan Kuban got his start in the village of Kuban singing and playing percussion "like any other Nubian boy," as he once put it, and serenading passengers on boats traveling the Nile. . . .

In 1942, Kuban moved to Cairo. . . . By then, he had also learned to play clarinet and *girba* (bagpipes) and begun to get work as a musician. . . . Kuban had an epiphany when he heard a jazz band from Harlem performing at Cairo's Gezira Sporting Club. The blended sounds of trombone, saxophone, clarinet and guitar and drums was a revelation, and he instantly wanted to experiment along those lines himself. . . . [In] 1949, Kuban began to work the clubs in Cairo, Alexandria and Aswan, revamping the old music with sax, electric guitar, bass, organ, trumpet and accordion. . . .

Later on, when the "world music" phenomenon began to bubble up in Europe and the U.S., Kuban brought his modern take on Nubian culture to the world. He made his international debut at Berlin's Heimatklaenge festival in 1989, and went on to perform widely. . . . Employing over 60 musicians and operating seven bands, Kuban continued playing traditional and popular music for both urban and rural Nubian enclaves in Cairo until he died there from a heart attack in June, 2001.

By making the most of tough street talk and a flippant attitude toward respectable society, Ahmed Adaweyah became the first star of shaabi in 1971.

Over the years, his songs, covering topics from romantic desire to the 1991 Gulf War in Kuwait and Iraq, earned him the enmity of government officials.

However, even as authorities officially banned Adaweyah's music, millions of his controversial cassettes were snapped up by the public.

In the 1990s, shaabi underwent another transformation as singers such as Shabaan Abdul Raheem, Sami Ali, and Sahar Hamdy combined the style with rap influences. Their profane and sexually explicit lyrics keep them off Egyptian radio and television but push their cassette sales over the hundred thousand mark.

Al-jil Music

Not all artists thrive on controversy, so another, more commercial, style of Egyptian music has emerged in Cairo since the 1980s. Known as *al-jil*, or "generation music," this style was invented by those who tired of listening to Western pop and wanted to put their own stamp on popular music. Al-jil performers are highly trained male and female vocalists who radiate sex appeal much the way movie stars do in the United States. Al-jil music features catchy melodies, slick production, and hypnotic techno beat rhythms.

Al-jil is popular among the burgeoning population of young people in the Arab world where, in some nations, three-quarters of the population is under the age of twenty-five. While not as shocking as shaabi, al-jil nonetheless promotes a spirit of rebellion in places where conservative religious leaders hold great power.

Amr Diab, born in Port Said, Egypt, was the first artist to take al-jil international. In the 1990s, Diab fused styles such as flamenco, rai, shaabi, and Egyptian pop with Arabic rhythms to form what has come to be called Pan Mediterranean music. The handsome Diab, dressed in his trademark billowing silk shirts and loose vests, became the first Arab artist to make high-quality music videos in 1992. His telegenic qualities led to a successful movie career in Egyptian films. In 1996 Diab's song "Nour el Ain" ("You Are the Light in My Eyes") sold over five hundred thousand copies immediately on its release and went on to become the biggest-selling Arabic recording of all time. As one of the best-selling world music artists, Diab now garners top billing at Egyptian and world music festivals.

Master Musicians of Morocco

Even as singers such as Diab play Arabic music that has been modernized, some Westerners have found beauty in music that is played in much the same way as it was centuries ago. For example, in Morocco, world music fans have found a wealth of inspiring music whose beauty lies in its unchanged, ancient roots.

One of the oldest styles was first popularized in the West in the late 1960s by Brian Jones, a guitarist with the Rolling Stones. Jones traveled to Morocco's Rif Mountains, where he heard a brotherhood of players called the Master Musicians of Jajouka perform music that featured a droning *ghaita*, a double-reed horn similar to the oboe, accompanied by chanting and drumming. The Master Musicians performed at ancient rituals dedicated to Pan, the Greek god of forests, fields, and flocks. These ceremonies sometimes lasted for days and the music, along with dance, was used to induce trance states that were meant to transform the consciousness and allow observers to communicate with supernatural worlds.

Jones discovered the Master Musicians of Jajouka during the hippie era, when he, along with millions of other Westerners, was taking hallucinogenic drugs believed to expand the consciousness. Jones recorded the musicians and took the tapes back to England, where he added psychedelic studio effects in the hopes that listeners could experience the mysticism of the Pan ceremonies. The *Pipes of Jajouka* album was released to mixed reviews in 1970, after Jones's death. In 1990 American bassist and composer Bill Laswell traveled back to the Rif Mountains with digital recording equipment and produced another album featuring the Master Musicians of Jajouka. This album introduced the ancient brotherhood of musicians to the world music

Brian Jones of the Rolling Stones recorded the Master Musicians of Jajouka in Morocco and produced an album of their music entitled The Pipes of Jajouka.

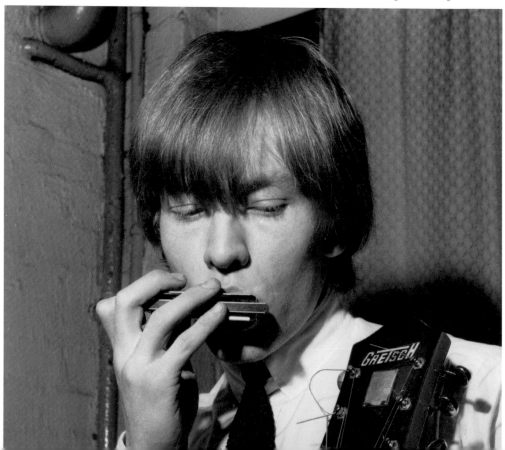

Music of Israel

As citizens of the only non-Islamic nation in the region, the Jewish people of Israel have produced a body of music with unique perspectives. Among the best known of Israeli world musicians is Yair Dalal, whose biography appears on yairdalal.com:

Yair Dalal, composer, violinist and oud player is probably the most prolific Israeli ethnic musician today. . . . Much of Dalal's output reflects the strong affinity he has for the desert and its habitants. Dalal's family came to Israel from Baghdad and he has included much Iraqi material in his work to date. Whether working on his own, or with his Alol ensemble, Dalal creates new Middle Eastern music by interweaving the traditions of Iraqi and Jewish Arabic music with a range of influences originating from such diverse cultural milieus as the Balkans to India. The evocative compositions comprise a unique and colorful sound. Dalal's musicianship is truly independent of time or trends. . . . Dalal also uses his extensive array of skills to span musical genres in performing his own compositions rooted in this musical tradition and inspired by the desert. . . .

Yair Dalal is a peace activist in all means; besides his musical endeavors, he devotes much time and energy to helping to remove ideological barriers between people and musicians from different cultures and, in particular between Jews and Arabs. He is collaborating with Palestinian musicians from the Middle East and has initiated and formed many peace projects.

market for the first time, and the group has since been a big draw at world music festivals.

Other Arab nations, besides Morocco, such as Iraq, Iran, Turkey, and Saudi Arabia, have their own musical traditions that date back centuries. Although most of this indigenous music is enjoyed by locals, a market for these sounds is growing among immigrants in Europe, North America, and elsewhere. With the world music market expanding faster than that of any other genre, sounds that were once heard only by a few thousand people in an isolated rural village can now be downloaded from the Internet. In this new era, sounds both old and new have become part of a modern music explosion.

Chapter Four

Music of India and the Far East

India and nations of the Far East have civilizations dating back more than six thousand years and societies that have long valued poetry, song, and dance. India is the second most densely populated nation on earth, and the musicians among its 1.1 billion people play thousands of musical styles that have developed over the centuries. In south India, music associated with Hindu teachings dates back to 5000 B.C., while throughout the nation hundreds of vastly dissimilar folk styles have evolved. This ancient music features rhythms, melodies, and instruments largely unfamiliar to Western ears, and is often based on esoteric concepts of philosophy and religion understood by few outside the region.

Ironically, while much of the nation's music remains unknown to Westerners, classical music from India was some of the first world music heard in the West. In the 1960s, the rock band the Beatles began featuring the twenty-string sitar in songs such as "Norwegian Wood" and

"Within You Without You." The instrument appeared on the record because of a musical collaboration between Beatle guitarist George Harrison and India's most renowned sitar player, Ravi Shankar. Since the Beatles were the era's most popular rock band, other groups, such as the Rolling Stones and Traffic, added sitar to their rock songs in imitation. In 1967 Harrison invited Shankar to perform at the seminal Monterey Pop Festival in California. When the film of the concert, *Monterey Pop*, was released the following year, Shankar became the most famous Indian musician in the West, and his record sales increased dramatically. Two years later Shankar performed at the Woodstock Music and Art Fair in Bethel, New York, at the time the largest and most successful rock festival in history.

"The Unique Aura of a Raga"

The sitar fad faded after a few years in the West. However, the raga music played by Shankar is nearly two thousand years old, with roots in the Vedic hymns of the Hindu religion. Although Shankar has performed with rock and jazz musicians, raga differs from Western music in several significant ways. Western music often uses ensembles of instruments to play harmony and chords (several complementary notes played simultaneously). Raga, however, is based on a single melody line played by a soloist who is backed by a droning note, played on a stringed instrument called a *tanpura*, and a rhythm played on tabla drums. Raga is also set apart from Western music because of its spiritual roots, as Shankar writes on his homepage:

To us, music can be a spiritual discipline on the path to self-realization, for we follow the traditional teaching that sound is God— [named] Nada Brahma: By this

process individual consciousness can be elevated to a realm of awareness where the revelation of the true meaning of the universe —its eternal and unchanging essence—can be joyfully experienced. Our ragas are the vehicles by which this essence can be perceived.[26]

Because of this history steeped in ancient religious philosophy, the complexities of ragas can take a lifetime to learn. An exploration of the musical structures of ragas clearly demonstrate why Shankar is one of the few living masters of the form.

The melodies of ragas are based on seventy-two *melas*, or sets of notes that are always played in the same order. Each mela may be played with nine different emotions or sentiments. These are described by Shankar as: "Shringara (romantic and erotic);

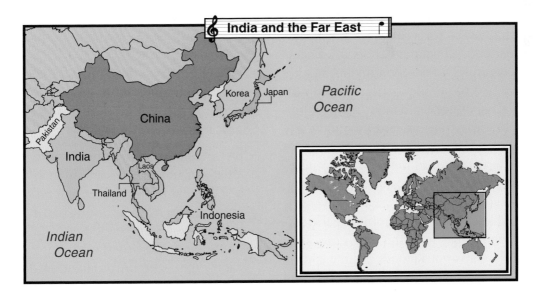

George Harrison (left) of the Beatles helped introduce Indian musician Ravi Shankar (right) to American and European audiences in the 1960s.

Hasya (humorous); Karuna (pathetic); Raudra (anger); Veera (heroic); Bhayanaka (fearful); Vibhatsa (disgustful); Adbhuta (amazement); Shanta (peaceful)."[27] These sentiments, in turn, are tied to moods associated with India's six seasons: winter, spring, summer, rainy season, autumn, and early winter. Ragas are also specific to eight different times of the day: early morning (before dawn), sunrise, morning, noon, afternoon, sunset, early evening, and late night. By combining the six-dozen melas with the nine emotions, the eight various moods of time and six seasons, Hindu scholars have estimated

that there can be nearly thirty-five thousand raga permutations. However, in practice, only about two hundred are commonly played.

Whatever the number, ragas are considered to be much more than mathematical arrangements of notes, as Shankar writes:

[A] raga is the projection of the artist's inner spirit, a manifestation of his most profound sentiments and sensibilities brought forth through tones and melodies. The musician must breathe life into each raga as he unfolds and expands it. . . . The unique aura of a raga (one might say its "soul") is its spiritual quality and manner of expression, and this cannot be learned from any book.[28]

The music created by the tabla player is nearly as important as that of the sitarist. The *dayan* tabla, or right-hand drum, is made from metal while the *bayan*, or left-hand bass drum, is made from wood. The heads of both are made from animal skin but have a center reinforced with a dried paste of iron filings and flour. Although tabla consist of two small drums played with the fingertips and thumbs, they are capable of producing both rhythm, called *tala*, and melodies, or *rag*.

"Intense Beauty, Loudly Acclaimed"

When three musicians play ragas in a concert, they follow tradition. First, the performers come onto the stage and tune their instruments for many minutes in front of the audience. This can lead to confusion among Western-ers who are unfamiliar with Indian music. In 1971 Shankar played with Harrison, Bob Dylan, Eric Clapton, and others at the Concert for Bangladesh, a benefit concert. After he spent some time tuning up onstage, his instrument was silent as he was about to begin the first song. However, the crowd burst into a round of exu-berant applause. Shankar leaned over to the microphone and said, "If you appreciate the tuning so much, I hope you'll enjoy the playing more."[29]

After the tuning, the recital begins with a soloist playing a section called an *alap*, described by Robert Maycock and Ken Hunt in *World Music Volume 1: Africa, Europe and the Middle East:*

In a fine alap the singer or player will conjure up phrase after phrase of intense beauty, loudly ac-claimed by ardent followers. . . . Feedback from the audience is im-portant, and a gesture or eye con-tact returned from a listener who obviously appreciates the music is highly valued. . . . As the alap pro-gresses, ornamentation grows more complex or flamboyant, the intensity builds, and a climactic high note is achieved—a moment whose emotional and musical power is greater for the long, long delay. The music winds down briefly, and then introduces a slow, almost lazy pulse for the so-called jor section. The speed of ar-ticulation gradually increases, melody evolves, and the pace stirs. Rhythmic animation follows, and the speed steps up in discreet stages. There is a brilliant climax, the music stops and everybody ap-plauds. Still, though, the percus-sionist sits silent.[30]

During the next section, called the *gat*, the tabla player begins, setting the rhythm for the music that follows. The player may also take a short drum solo while the sitarist remains silent. During the gat, the pace and intensity of the music incrementally increase until the

Anoushka Shankar: Continuing a Tradition

Few sitarists alive can compete with Ravi Shankar. However, the sitar master's daughter Anoushka, born in London in 1981, has been trained to carry on the tradition, as the "Anoushka Shankar" Web site explains:

Anoushka Shankar . . . is the only artist in the world to be trained completely by her father and legendary sitar virtuoso and composer, Ravi Shankar. She has been playing and studying the sitar with him since she was nine, and at age thirteen she made her performing debut in New Delhi, India. That same year, Anoushka entered the recording studio for the first time to play on her father's recording, *In Celebration.* Two years later she helped as conductor with her father and dear friend, George Harrison, on the 1997 Angel release, *Chants of India.* Shortly thereafter she signed an exclusive contract with Angel/EMI Classics. In the Fall of 1998 her first solo recording, *Anoushka,* was released to tremendous critical acclaim. Two albums followed, *Anourag* in 2000 and *Live at Carnegie Hall in 2001.* The latter was nominated for a Grammy Award in the Best World Music Album category, making her the youngest ever nominee in that category. . . .

Ravi Shankar's daughter, Anoushka Shankar, has won acclaim for her music.

Anoushka has shared the stage with many of the world's top celebrities, including Sting, Madonna, Nina Simone, Anjelique Kidjo, Herbie Hancock, Elton John, Peter Gabriel and James Taylor. . . . As her solo career continues to blossom, it seems she is poised to carry forward her father's legacy as one of the most creative and influential figures in the music world.

song peaks in a climax called a *jhala*. At the end, the sitarist and drummer begin a musical conversation, trading musical phrases and imitating and building off one another. Skilled tabla players can make their drums "talk," or imitate speech, while sitar players may drop in pieces of other ragas or play counter-rhythms to the tablas.

Popular Sounds of Bollywood

While traditional music has a long, rich history in India, the most popular songs coming from the subcontinent today are called *filmi*, film music, or cine music. In a nation of more than a billion people where only 55 million households have televisions, the cinema is the primary form of entertainment for most Indians. To provide product for this huge audience, the film industry in Bombay (now called Mumbai) has grown into the largest in the world. As the Hollywood of India, the industry, jokingly nicknamed Bollywood, produces twice as many films annually as the U.S. film industry, and sells a billion more tickets.

With very few exceptions, nearly every picture made in Bollywood is a musical film with story lines about love, romance, heartbreak, virtuous heroes, and vanquished villains. Actors break into song in nearly every scene, and each movie has five to twenty song-and-dance numbers, some that feature dozens of elaborately costumed performers. The music is a mixture of sounds that can incorporate styles as diverse as traditional Indian religious melodies and American Broadway musicals, as David B. Reck explains in *Worlds of Music:*

> Cine music is a curious and sometimes bizarre blend of East and West: choppy and hyperactive melodies, often in "oriental" scales, are belted out by nasal singers over Latin rhythms and an eclectic accompaniment that may include a trap [drum] set, electric organs and guitars, violins, xylophones, celeste [a keyboard with metal plates that produce bell-like tones], bongos, sitar, tabla, or bamboo flute. More recently some genres of Indian pop music have been crafted to sound exactly like their Western pop counterparts, only their lyrics in Indian languages [make] them distinguishable from the latest hit tune. The lyrics of cine songs tend to focus on the eternal trivia and complications of love and romance.[31]

In films, these songs appear to be sung by India's most famous young actors and actresses. However, the stars are actually lip-synching to music blasted through loudspeakers on the movie set. The real vocalists, some of them over seventy years old, are called playback singers and are never seen in the movies.

The most well-known female playback singers are two sisters, Asha Bhosle, born in 1929, and Lata Mangeshkar, born in 1934. Working in an industry that churns out hundreds of movies a year, Mangeshkar has sung in over eighteen hundred films and worked with 165 composers. She is identified in the *Guinness Book of World Records* as the world's most recorded singer, having recorded thirty thousand songs in twenty Indian languages since 1948.

While Bhosle falls slightly short of that record, she shares a common talent with her sister: the ability to convince an audience that the song she is singing is coming out of the mouth of a beautiful young actress on the screen. Few singers in their seventies can match that feat. A *Los Angeles Times* review of Bhosle's June 2005 concert in Long Beach, California, reveals why the vocalist is known as the "golden voice of Bollywood." As reporter Don Heckman writes:

[Bhosle's] voice was a thing of wonder—crystal clear in the upper range, warm and smoky in her chest tones, the notes flowing with consummate ease across the octaves. At times sounding young and girlish, she switched easily into mature, womanly tones. . . . Four hardworking dancers whipped through several costume changes and choreography ranging from Indian classical styles to hip-hop. . . . But it was Bhosle's versatility that took the performance up a level, well beyond the Bollywood pop glitz. Starting her set with a kind of Indian rap, she moved on to incorpo-

rate gorgeous balladry, jazz-tinged scat singing and a brief foray into classical Indian ghazal singing. And she did it all superbly.[32]

Bhosle and other Bollywood vocalists sing songs written by highly trained, mostly male composers, called musical directors, who are also extremely prolific. These people work under intense pressure and may work on as many as thirty films at once, requiring them to write upwards of three hundred songs in a few months. Unable to wait for inspiration to strike, directors often copy—some say plagiarize—Western pop, native folk songs, and religious songs called *qawwali*.

The most famous Bollywood musical director is A.R. Rahman who, in addition to writing for films, collaborated on the musical play *Bombay Dreams* with British producer Andrew Lloyd Webber. While Rahman's music is considered to be among the best by world music critics, other directors do not fare as well, as Chris Nickson writes in *The NPR Curious Listener's Guide to World Music*:

If Rahman represents what might be called the high, sophisticated end of *filmi*, then . . . many others, [occupy the pretentious] kitsch corner. The vocal melodies are always strong—as they have to be for Bollywood—but the arrangements can verge on the ridiculous. It's not uncommon to have shades of heavy metal, synth pop, techno,

The crystal clear voice of Asha Bhosle is heard in many Indian movies.

and sitar and tabla cheek by jowl in the same song. Without doubt, it makes for fun listening, quite addictive in its own way, and this is the side of Bollywood that's generally been captured on recent compilations and the one that's attracted Western listeners through its novelty. But for all the apparent random [blending] of musical elements, there's always a fierce intelligence behind it.[33]

While critics may scoff at some Bollywood music, it is incredibly popular in India, where the latest movie hits are heard blasting from restaurants, nightclubs, taxicabs, and market vendor stalls. Outside India, the music first became popular with non-Indian world music fans in England in the 1980s. Bollywood music has also been growing in popularity in the United States since the 2003 release of the movie *Bollywood/Hollywood*, which exposed many Americans to the musical style for the first time.

Bhangra Goes British

Audiences in Great Britain have popularized another style of Indian music called bhangra, which has roots in the northwestern region of Punjab on the Pakistan border. Traditionally, bhangra is dance music that is played on a large barrel-like drum called a *dhol* at harvest celebrations. Skilled drummers beat one side of the drum with a heavy stick while lightly tapping the

Bhangra is Indian dance music played on a large drum called a dhol. *Here, Johnny Kalsi performs with a* dhol *in 2004 in England.*

Music from the Roof of the World

The mountain nation of Tibet is the home of Buddhism, a religion with a strong emphasis on spiritual music. Native Tibetans have been tragically repressed since 1950 when China annexed the country and destroyed over six thousand ancient Buddhist temples. In recent years, however, Tibetan music has been popularized in the West, which has helped Tibet's political situation remain in the public eye. Chris Nickson explains in The NPR Curious Listener's Guide to World Music:

[It is] Tantric monks who've received most attention [from the world music community]. Having fled to India following [the 1950] Chinese occupation of Tibet, they continue to make their ancient music, with its multitonal sound, called gyü-ke, that emphasizes the overtones and harmonics of the notes. The Gyuto Monks Tantric Choir is the most widely recorded example, championed by musicians like drummer Mickey Hart of the Grateful Dead on albums like *Freedom Chants from the Roof of the World*. There's a true spiritual depth to this meditative music, which has found favor with both world music and New Age fans as well as helped other Tibetan artists like Nawang Khechog.

Tibet also has secular music, of course, and Yungchen Llamo has been a recent success story. She escaped the country by traveling on foot over the Himalayas [to India]. Her debut album, *Tibet*, allowed her glorious voice to shine unaccompanied, while the follow-up framed it in subtle modern textures. She's become a favorite at festivals around the world, but, more important, she keeps awareness of Tibet and the political situation high.

Gyuto monks keep the ancient music of Tibet alive.

other drumhead with a slender flexible rod called a switch. This produces a loping swing rhythm that imitates the sound of a farmer harvesting grain with a scythe. It is also a rhythm that immigrant Punjabi musicians in a group called Alaap used as a basis for a new style of dance music in Great Britain in the late 1970s.

Alaap used a violin, accordion, acoustic guitar, dhol, and tabla to record *Teri Chunni De Sitare*, an album that had a major impact on the Indian community in Great Britain. The press, sensing the next big thing in music, popularized the sound, inspiring dozens of groups to form to meet the sudden demand for bhangra. By the early 1980s, discos featuring live bhangra bands often were attended by more than two thousand people, many of them second- or third-generation British Punjabis.

In the years that followed, the ancient beat of the dhol drum was easily adapted to drum machines, while synthesizers took the place of accordions. By the late 1990s, bands such as the Safri Boys were mixing Punjabi lyrics with digital samples and rave beats for a thoroughly modern style of bhangra. Having evolved into an electronic dance music, bhangra is undergoing constant change at the hands of musicians and producers who make music they hope will be relevant to a young audience that demands new sounds.

An Impact on World Music

India is not the only Asian nation with a rich musical heritage. China, Indonesia, Korea, Laos, Thailand, and other countries in the region also have song traditions that are thousands of years old. Japan has the world's largest music industry after the United States, and produces thousands of records annually that cater to national tastes. Indian music, however, has made the largest impact on the world music scene. Since Ravi Shankar first dazzled Western audiences in the 1960s, several of India's numerous musical styles have found popularity in the West. With its dizzying profusion of music, there is little doubt that India will continue to influence musicians throughout the world for many years to come.

Chapter Five

Celtic Music and the Sounds of Eastern Europe

Anumber of European nations have been essential to the world music revolution, contributing dozens of unique musical traditions to the genre. The indigenous European music has developed over thousands of years on a broad swath of land that stretches from Ireland in the west to Siberia in the east. In countless regions in between, people have developed their own folk, religious, and classical music that today may be heard blended with rock and roll, soul, funk, rap, and numerous other permutations of modern sound.

With a population that speaks dozens of languages and dialects, Europeans have a broad range of native music to draw on. In addition, easy access to modern media, recording technology,

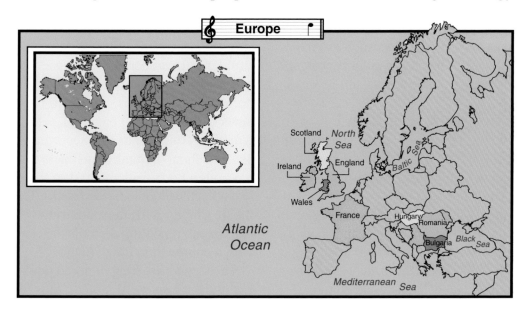

An Irish piper holds a set of pipes, an instrument frequently used in traditional Celtic music.

The Celts were eventually conquered by Roman and German invaders, and in later centuries, the Anglo-Saxons. Although their culture was absorbed by others, the Celtic language, also known as Gaelic, survived over the centuries, especially in Ireland, Scotland, and Wales. Celtic mythology has also been handed down from generation to generation and this folklore has provided knowledge about the ancient music, which is divided into three forms. One form of the music is meant to aid sleep or meditation, another is for happy moments, and a third branch is for lamentation, expressions of grief and mourning. These characteristics, according to June Skinner Sawyers in *Celtic Music: A Complete Guide*, allow for music "that evokes emotions of sadness, joy, sorrow or delight. . . . a [unique Celtic] spirit that transcends time, distance, and political units."[34]

and musical instruments gives European musicians a decided advantage over players in places such as Africa, who must often battle poverty, war, and disease to make their music.

The Celtic Tradition

The most popular form of world music to emerge from Europe is also one of the oldest. Celtic music has its roots in ancient tribes who lived in Ireland, Scotland, Wales, and the Brittany region in France between 2000 B.C. and about the fifth century A.D. Although these people were of different tribes, they shared a related language, music, and culture.

Celtic music was originally played on an assortment of pipes, horns, stringed instruments, and percussion instruments. In modern times, these various instruments include fiddles, mandolins, guitars, harps, flutes, uilleann pipes (a type of small bagpipe), pennywhistles, concertinas and accordions, and a bodhran (a frame drum made with a wooden body and a goatskin head, played with a double-headed stick). The music played with these instruments has strong, repeating melodies backed with a compelling, fixed rhythm.

The Celts have long honored poetry and the spoken word, and ballads, or sung narrative poems, are popular in Celtic music. Other musical styles are based on folk dances such as jigs, reels, hornpipes, polkas, and slow instrumental pieces called airs.

An Irish Milestone

Although the style has roots in ancient times, Celtic music remained obscure for thousands of years. While it was kept alive by a few traditionalists and

The Ancient Musical Connection

Although Celtic music developed in isolation on the British Isles, it shares similar characteristics with ancient musical forms from other lands. June Skinner Sawyers explains in Celtic Music: A Complete Guide:

Much of traditional Celtic music is pentatonic. Pentatonic refers to a scale that has five tones to the octave. On the piano the pentatonic scale can be reproduced by playing only the black keys. And yet the total pentatonic scale occurs in the music of nearly all ancient cultures—China, Polynesia, Africa —as well as that of the Native Americans and the Celtic peoples. . . . Scottish-music scholar John Purser has noted the similarity between Gaelic [Celtic] psalm-singing and Middle Eastern chanting; in particular, he compared the music of a Christian community in

Ethiopia and a Christian community in the western Highlands [in Scotland] and arrived at some rather startling conclusions. Despite having no direct or indirect contact with one another for hundreds of years, "if at all," the two solo chants use the same pentatonic scale, in exactly the same manner; the . . . main notes are "almost identical and the pace of delivery is the same."

His explanation? "The best that can be suggested is that the Gaelic-speaking people . . . retained a style of singing with roots in very ancient chant.". . . As further proof of the link between East and West, remember that the pentatonic scale is also the basis of Chinese music. . . . Hence, the traditional music of the Celtic lands share much common ground with the folk music of Eastern Europe, Asia, Africa, and the Middle East.

folklorists, the music was rarely played in public. This situation began to change in 1960 with innovations by Irish harpsichordist and composer Sean Ó Riada, born John Reidy in Cork County. Ó Riada wrote music for the documentary film *I Am Ireland*, a soundtrack that combined traditional Celtic songs with orchestral music. In 1963 Ó Riada took the visionary step of transforming his orchestra, Ceoltóirí Chualann, from a classical chamber ensemble to one that played traditional music with flutes, fiddles, an accordion, uilleann pipes, and a harp. Although the band was together only for a short while, it was a catalyst for a new era in Celtic music.

While playing with Ceoltóirí Chualann, master piper Paddy Moloney was invited to record an instrumental album for a new Dublin-based record company. Moloney put together a band called the Chieftains that featured musicians playing the tin whistle, fiddle, concertina, and bodhran. As Geoff Wallis and Sue Wilson write in *The Rough Guide to Irish Music*, the resulting album, also called *The Chieftains*, was an "Irish milestone . . . [whose] spirited immediacy and stripped down authenticity . . . was little short of revelatory. Moloney's arrangements of traditional airs and dance tunes were strongly influenced by Ó Riada's technique of spotlighting different instruments within a group format, as well as his use of harmony, eschewing pop inflections to focus on the tunes' inherent vitality and beauty."[35]

In the following years, the Chieftains went from local celebrities to international Celtic superstars. Among the group's fans were Beatle bassist Paul McCartney, Rolling Stones vocalist Mick Jagger, and even Pope John Paul II, who invited the group to play before an audience of 1.35 million in Dublin's

The Celtic superstar group The Chieftains brought Irish music to the masses.

Phoenix Park in 1979. During this time, Moloney continued to innovate, writing songs such as "Bonaparte's Retreat," a fourteen-minute suite about French emperor Napoleon Bonaparte. In 1982 the Chieftains opened for the Rolling Stones in Dublin and the following year they were the first group ever to play on the Great Wall of China. In the 1990s, the group broke new ground, recording *The Long Black Veil*, an album of traditional tunes sung by the biggest stars in rock and roll, including Sting, Jagger, and Sinéad O'Connor. Collaborators on other albums included Elvis Costello, Van Morrison, and Jackson Browne.

In 2005 the Chieftains celebrated forty-two years together. Although their impact on Celtic music cannot be over-estimated today, Moloney recalls a time when few people were aware of the Irish musical heritage:

> There was no shortage of [traditional] musicians. . . . There was a shortage of listeners. [The music] was being played. It just wasn't being heard. . . . I never believed [the Chieftains] would take off. . . . But like Martin Luther King, I had a dream. Now Irish music has soared throughout the world. I'm tremendously proud of that.[36]

While bringing Irish music to the masses, Moloney and the Chieftains blazed a trail for many young musicians who have been able to explore their Celtic musical roots. Mary Black,

for example, has been using her beautiful, expressive voice to sing songs that blend elements of Celtic music with rock and soul since 1982. From 1980 to 1996, the Pogues blended punk rock sensibilities with ancient Celtic ballads. And in the twenty-first century, Sharon Shannon has used her talents on the accordion to play energetic Irish dance standards and new material in the old Celtic style.

Celtic Tunes in Great Britain

While the Irish led the way, the Celtic revival also blossomed in Great Britain where folk festivals were very popular in the late 1960s. These musical concerts brought together a wide range of musicians from the Celtic world. In 1971 the Boys of the Lough, a group composed of two Irish and two Scottish players, were the hit of the Newcastle Folk Festival. Driven by Aly Bain's high-energy Celtic fiddle playing and Mike Whelan's singing and guitar playing, the group released their eponymous first album in 1972. As Wallis and Wilson write, this album "introduced [the band] as the not-too-distant cousins of the Chieftains in terms of their sensitive arrangements and concentration on bringing out the instruments' natural colors—the application of such refined technique to traditional tunes being a notably innovative tactic."[37] After the Boys of the Lough made their mark in Great Britain, they brought their Celtic music to the American folk scene in the 1970s. Since that time the Boys of the

Mike Heron (left) and the Scottish group the Incredible String Band blended traditional Celtic music with acid rock.

Lough have played fifty-four tours of the United States.

Folk festivals also played an important role in exposing Celtic musicians to American performers. Bluegrass mandolin player Bill Monroe was particularly popular in Great Britain because his music has Celtic origins: Bluegrass is based on music played by Scottish settlers in the Appalachian Mountains in the nineteenth century, and the instrumentation and lyrics of the style have much in common with Celtic balladry.

Singer and songwriter Bob Dylan was another musical influence from the United States. At the time, Dylan was fusing traditional blues and country with rock and roll into a form called folk rock or country rock. This melding of two styles proved to be an inspiration to Scottish groups such as the Incredible String Band, who mixed elements of traditional Celtic music with acid rock. Around the same time, the band Pentangle drew upon influences such as blues, rock, folk, jazz, Celtic sounds, and even Indian music to create an influential and eclectic sound.

These innovations were not confined to traditionally Celtic regions. In England, Fairport Convention, inspired by American folk rock, drew upon Celtic roots to invent unique folks songs that, while new, sounded as if they were written in past centuries. Sawyers describes one composition by vocalist Sandy Denny:

To many of her fans [Sandy Denny] was the voice of Fairport, a honeycombed jewel equally at home with older and contemporary material. But it was with the traditional that she shone her brightest. Even Denny originals like "Fotheringay," about the [sixteenth-century] imprisonment of Mary, Queen of Scots, in Fotheringay Castle on the eve of her execution, sound as if they emerged full blown from the Middle Ages, so thoroughly and yet naturally were they conceived. With its harpsichordlike guitars and angelic background harmonies, the song could easily be thought an authentic piece of sacred medieval music.[38]

Denny, who died tragically after falling down a flight of stairs in 1978, was among the many talents who played with Fairport Convention. Singer, songwriter, and guitarist Richard Thompson pursued a solo career with his wife, Linda, in the 1970s and continues to play today. Bassist Ashley Hutchings went on to form another seminal Celtic group, Steeleye Span.

Like Fairport Convention, Steeleye Span has a female vocalist, Maddy Prior, who mesmerizes fans with her emotive, soaring voice. Members of Steeleye Span also write inventive and original songs based on English and Celtic folklore. In a move away from the acoustic instruments used by Fair-port, however, the band uses electric guitars and drums in the manner of a rock band, creating a unique British version of country rock. Although the band has undergone personnel changes, Steeleye Span continues to market CDs in the world music genre and play folk festivals throughout the world.

Celtic Progressive and New Age

Fairport Convention, Pentangle, and Steeleye Span had a profound influence on young musicians. Today, a thriving Celtic-progressive music scene exists in Dublin, Edinburgh, and London, where players fuse jazz, African rhythms, acid rock, and other styles. Members of Mouth Music sing in Gaelic while backed by African percussion and digital dance tracks. Shooglenifty mixes up Celtic fiddles and mandolins with a kaleidoscopic array of rhythms from West Africa and the Caribbean. The eight-piece Afro Celt Sound System, as the name implies, combines sounds and instruments from two eclectic regions. With musicians of Irish, Kenyan, Senegalese, and Guinean heritage, the group plays a distinctly danceable music with keyboards, African talking drums, koras, the Irish harp, uilleann pipes, bongos, banjos, and programmed beats.

Computers are often used in Celtic new age music, a genre that at times has eclipsed the traditional style. The rise of Celtic new age may be traced directly to Enya Brennan (Eithne Ní Bhraonáin, in Gaelic), an Irish singer and composer. Her debut 1987 album *Enya* featured the singer's delicate vocals, the uilleann pipes, guitar, piano, and drum machine to create a masterpiece of ethereal music that single-handedly launched the Celtic new age sound.

Enya's records sold in the millions and influenced others to follow her path to stardom. Canadian-born Loreena McKennitt has sold nearly as many albums as Enya, with cross-cultural musical explorations into Celtic, Asian, Spanish, and even Native American influences.

Led by McKennitt and Enya, by 2000 Celtic music made up two-thirds of the entries on *Billboard*'s top world music albums chart. Celtic music festivals are also extremely popular with annual summer gatherings like Nova Scotia's Celtic Colours, Glasgow's Celtic Connections, and Brittany's Festival Interceltique.

Music of Eastern Europe

Although Celtic acts often dominate the world music charts, a wide array of sounds comes from continental Europe. Like that of the Celts, this music varies from indigenous folk music to traditional sounds that have been updated with African beats, electronic instruments, and hip-hop sensibilities.

Although Germany, France, Italy, and Spain have produced many styles over the years, most of the European music marketed under the world music genre is from eastern Europe. These nations, between the Baltic Sea and Russia, are not unified geographically or ethnically, but most suffered under the

Celtic new age music became popular primarily due to the recordings and performances of singer Enya Brennan (left).

Enya's New Age Celts

No one has been more responsible for what *Entertainment Weekly* called the "Celtification" of pop music than Irish singer Enya, the top-selling solo musician in Ireland and a pioneer of the Celtic new age genre. Born in County Donegal, Ireland, in 1961, Enya grew up in a musical family. Her siblings and two uncles formed the groundbreaking Celtic group Clannad in the 1970s, and Enya began playing keyboards and singing backing vocals with the band in 1980.

In 1982 Enya joined forces with ex-Clannad producer Nicky Ryan and his wife, Roma. Together they launched Enya's solo career with Nicky producing and Roma writing lyrics to Enya's ethereal melodies. In 1986 BBC television commissioned Enya and the Ryans to create music for a television documentary called *The Celts*. In 1987 the music was released as *Enya*, the artist's debut album.

In 1988 Enya achieved a major breakthrough with the song "Orinoco Flow" on the album *Watermark*. Played repeatedly on British radio stations, the song caught on with world music fans in the United States. In the following decade, over 8 million copies of *Watermark* were sold. In 1991 her follow-up album, *Shepherd Moons*, sold 10 million copies and earned the singer a Grammy Award for best new age album. Four years later, Enya won another for *The Memory of Trees*.

Although often classified as a new age artist, Enya considers her music to be of Celtic heritage. Some songs are sung entirely in Irish Gaelic, while Roma has written others that mix English, Latin, Welsh, Spanish, and even languages created by author J. R. R. Tolkien for his *Lord of the Rings* books.

rule of the Soviet Union between 1945 and 1989. Authoritarian leaders harshly suppressed musical experimentation, purged the airwaves of many types of ethnic music, and strictly controlled access to technologies such as recording equipment and musical duplication systems. The oppressive situation had a positive effect, however. Much of eastern European music is real folk music that exists in its original form because musicians were isolated from forbidden

Gypsy Music

Gypsies, or the Romany people, have long faced discrimination in Europe. However, their music is an important part of eastern European culture, as Chris Nickson writes in The NPR Curious Listener's Guide to World Music:

One of the historical roles of the Romany people has been as musicians (indeed, the image of the Gypsy violinist has become a romantic stereotype). In part, that's been because it was one of the few jobs available in societies that were habitually prejudiced against the Romany. So they made their living traveling around, playing for weddings, circumcisions, and dances. They needed to be familiar with many different styles and often imparted new ideas to local musicians, while also learning from them. . . .

It's the violin that people associate with Gypsies, however, and there's no shortage of that. From Sandor Fodor to the remarkable [group] Taraf de Haîdouks, the violin music can be quietly beautiful or wildly pulse pounding. . . .

There are also bands across the Balkans looking to the future. . . . Besh o Drom, for instance, employ traditional instruments but also use sampling and a DJ as part of their arsenal, integrating the techniques well to excellent effect. As with all folk traditions, constant reinvention keeps the music fresh. . . .

[There] are also some excellent Romany vocalists. Macedonian Esma Redzepova has emerged from her own country to claim an international following with her big, emotive voice. But it's Vera Bilá who's been anointed as the queen. . . . Adding soft Brazilian rhythms to Gypsy song, she's created a curious, attractive blend of the raw and the sophisticated as a backdrop for her intoxicating voice. Now she tours the world, although at home she and her band, Kale . . . still suffer prejudice because they're Gypsies.

music such as rock and roll, blues, jazz, and other sounds of the West.

A few isolated communist governments did sponsor traditional music, and Bulgaria, a small nation of about 7 million people, has produced one of the most unusual world music success stories. In the 1950s, the Soviet-backed

Bulgarian government organized the Bulgarian State Ensemble for Folk Songs and Dances. The artistic goal of the ensemble was to remake rough-hewn Bulgarian folk songs and imbue them with harmonies and arrangements that highlighted their distinctive, if unusual, tones and irregular rhythms. This work was achieved by musical director Philip Kutev, whose work is described by Kim Burton in *World Music: The Rough Guide:*

> His great gift was the ability to take the sounds of village singers, drone-based and full of close dissonances [disagreeable combinations of sounds] . . . and from this forge a musical language which answered the aesthetic demands of western European concepts of form and harmony without losing touch with the atmosphere of the original tunes.[39]

In 1952 the Bulgarian State Radio and Television Female Vocal Choir was founded with twenty-three singers from various rural regions of the country. They performed traditional Bulgarian folk songs that were rewritten to be sung in what Peter Spencer describes in *World Beat* as "distinctively hard, narrow tones, given an added resonance in the recording studio that results in sheets of sound interacting with aural space in unusual ways. [The] nasal tones, without discernable vibrato . . . join in dense chords, with [voices singing] five or six different intervals in a single octave."[40]

The unusual music prompted Swiss producer Marcel Cellier to begin recording the music in 1975. Spurning the clumsy, bureaucratic name State Radio and Television Female Vocal Choir, Cellier dubbed the choir Le Mystere des Voix Bulgares, or "the Mysterious Voices of Bulgaria." He recorded their music over the course of several years and released the songs on three separate CDs. The albums became surprise world music hits and are now considered classics. The recordings were followed by intensive concert tours of Le Mystere des Voix Bulgares in major halls in Europe, America, and Asia.

European Virtuosity

The Bulgarian choir is but one musical act from eastern Europe that used harmony and melody unfamiliar to the Western ear. In the Tuva region between Russia and Mongolia, the group Huun-Huur-Tu practices throat singing. A person who uses this ancient technique can sing multiple notes, or overtones, at the same time. And in Hungary, Romania, and elsewhere, Romany people perform music with virtuosity that is at varying times melancholic, sentimental, wild, and uninhibited. Thanks to folk traditions dating back two millennia, there is no shortage of world music from Europe. And with dozens of styles yet to be discovered by outsiders, European world music will no doubt continue to amaze and entertain for years to come.

Chapter Six

Music of the Caribbean

The islands of the Caribbean have long been the crossroads of many cultures. Spanish explorers first brought African slaves to present-day Jamaica, Puerto Rico, Cuba, and the Dominican Republic in the sixteenth century. In the centuries that followed, European nations, primarily Great Britain and France, gained control of various Caribbean islands. Like the Spanish, these colonizers depended on the forced labor of hundreds of thousands of black slaves to grow sugarcane and other crops.

The colonization of the Caribbean annihilated the native Taino Indians and other indigenous tribes. However, two percussion instruments have survived from the first American cultures. Maracas are shakers that are traditionally made with small gourds mounted on sticks and filled with pebbles or seeds. The guiro, or scraper, is a hollow gourd with parallel notches cut into it. This is played by a percussionist rubbing a wooden stick over the notches to pro-

duce a ratchetlike sound. Both instruments play central roles in modern Caribbean music.

Although the world will never hear the music played by the indigenous Caribbean people, most music fans are familiar with the exciting and diverse musical traditions such as calypso and reggae that have evolved over the years. This musical mix is a result of a clash of cultures, religions, and traditions. The Europeans brought their musical instruments and sounds from martial, classical, and religious genres to the islands. The slaves, most of them from West and Central Africa, brought their own instruments, dances, and musical heritage. Although the colonizers tried to suppress black musical customs, the slaves used their native cultural tools to mold and shape certain elements of European music into something that they could appreciate and understand. In doing so, black artists created new forms of music that allowed the enslaved people to defy their oppressors, as journalist Rubén Martinez writes on the "Havana: The Golden Era" Web page:

> If Africa and the ancient Americas had truly been conquered, everyone would perform and dance waltzes today. The grooves of tropical music on the [islands] . . . provide great catharsis, an affirmation of life itself, of cultural and spiritual survival.[41]

This music was developed in dozens of areas isolated from one another. The thirty islands of the Caribbean chain stretch over 2,500 miles (4,023km) and contain over 30 million people. In centuries past, black people were not readily able to travel. Thus, those who lived on an island ruled by Spain developed music that was different from those who were exposed to British or French society. As a result, Cuban music has its distinctly Spanish influences while Jamaican reggae has been affected by British culture.

The musical genres that developed in isolation began to change and grow after slavery was abolished in the nineteenth century. Interaction between the islanders increased as Haitians moved to Cuba, Jamaicans worked in the Dominican Republic, Cubans traveled to Trinidad, and so on. This led to further cross-pollination of musical styles, enhanced by the immigration of Chinese, Indians, and Arabs to the islands in the mid-1800s.

Cuba's Santeria Influences

Few islands can compete with Cuba when it comes to cross-cultural music development. The island is home to dances and musical styles, such as the rumba, the mambo, and the cha-cha, that fuse African and Spanish elements.

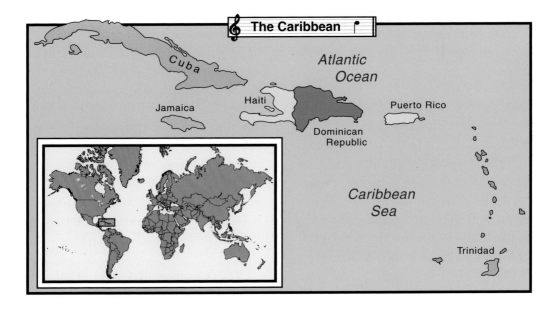

The Caribbean

Cuba

Atlantic Ocean

Jamaica

Haiti

Dominican Republic

Puerto Rico

Caribbean Sea

Trinidad

Drummers and dancers in Cuba perform toques *during a Santeria ceremony.*

These styles evolved in a country where slavery, repression, and poverty have remained nearly constant over the centuries.

Slavery was legal in Cuba longer than anywhere else in the Americas. By the time bonded servitude was abolished there in 1886, more than half the island's population consisted of blacks of Yoruba descent, people from the African nations of Benin, Nigeria, Congo, and Cameroon. Most of these black Cubans practiced a religion called Santeria that mixed the Yoruba belief in a variety of deities called orishas with certain Roman Catholic practices, especially the belief in saints.

Santeria, which is still practiced in Cuba and elsewhere, has had a powerful influence on the island's music. Believers say that each orisha may be called down to Earth by performances of specific drum patterns, called *toques*. These are played during rituals on thundering drums called *batá* and rattles called *shekere*. In *World Music: The Rough Guide*, Jan Fairley describes the importance of Santeria's religious music:

These complex rhythms are the heartbeat of Cuban music, working away beneath the Latin layers on top. The batás and shekere of the ceremonies crop up regularly in contemporary Cuban bands, and the physical and emotional intensity of musical performance in Cuba emanates in part from the power and potency of African ritual and its participatory nature. . . . The links between Afro-Cuban religions like Santeria and music-making remain close.[42]

Rumba Rhythms

The toques and dances performed during Santeria rituals were also popular in a nonreligious context. In the 1890s, sugar mill workers held community parties where Santeria drummers played a musical style called rumba, and dancers performed dances of the same name. (This style of music is not to be confused with the rhumba, a popular twentieth-century Latin dance performed in the United States and Europe.) Ed Morales describes the Cuban rumba in *The Latin Beat:*

> From the religious *toques* . . . evolved a more secular tradition of rumbas, popular gatherings in which revelers performed dances derived from Santeria rituals. . . . [Rumbas] are similar to *toques* in musical content but are less formal in their religious function. The *orishas* are praised, the centrality of drumming remains, but the celebration is not necessarily for initiates—it's more like a block party.[43]

There are three styles of rumba. The *yambú* is a slow dance usually enjoyed

A Cuban street band provides inspiration for an impromptu rumba in Havana.

by older couples. The *guaguancó* is a faster dance in which couples perform provocative moves such as pelvic thrusting. The *columbia* is a fast dance aggressively performed only by men, who often mimic combat by pretending to stab one another with knives.

Musicians performing rumba use a wide array of percussion instruments. Each song begins with a percussionist playing the clave, two wooden sticks used to tap out a rhythm that the rest of the musicians will follow throughout the song. For rumba songs, the clave player usually taps the sticks in a pattern of two beats followed by three beats. Other instruments play polyrhythms on various conga drums, iron shakers, wooden tubes played with sticks called *catas*, and even old packing crates beaten with drumsticks.

After the drums set the rhythm and get the crowd dancing, a rumba vocalist or duet will sing a long expressive melody, followed by a call and response in which a vocalist sings a line that is repeated by other singers. This is followed by a lead drummer beating a rowdy, improvised solo as the lead singer shouts out encouragement. As the rest of the band joins in the action, the song reaches a crowd-pleasing, frenzied section known as the *montuno*.

Son Sounds

Rumba remains popular in Cuba, and bands such as Los Muñequitos de Matanzas have been playing the music at public concerts for the past fifty years. However, another Cuban musical style, *son*, has garnered a huge international audience since 1997. This is largely due to a single album, *Buena Vista Social Club*, and a movie of the same name, which reintroduced son music to a worldwide audience.

The origins of Cuban son can be traced back to the nineteenth century, when the style was associated with Santiago, Cuba. Traditional son bands are led by several vocalists who sing together with strong harmonies. The singers are accompanied by a bass player and a musician who plays a guitarlike instrument called a *tres*, which has three strings each in a double set. As in rumba, a clave player sets the rhythm while complex counter-rhythms are played by maracas, bongos, and guiros. According to Morales, this lineup allows for "the juxtaposition of three rhythmic patterns: the *tumbao*, a syncopated bassline; the rhythm section, played by guitar, bongos, and maracas; and the clave [rhythm]."[44]

Son first attained wide popularity in Havana in the 1920s when the group Sexteto Habanero played sizzling-hot dance music featuring a pair of lead vocalists and a wailing trumpet. A series of records introduced the son music of Sexteto Habanero to the outside world. The music quickly became a fad in U.S. and European cities. The records also inspired musicians in Congo, Senegal, Mali, and elsewhere in Africa to introduce Cuban rhythms into their own sounds such as soukous.

By the 1940s, son orchestras were adding jazz improvisation and a swing-

Spicy Salsa

Cuban music is at the root of salsa, one of the most popular musical styles of recent decades. The style is a blending of Cuban son and rumba with other elements such as rock and roll, African American soul and funk, and Caribbean music including the Puerto Rican *plena* and the Dominican merengue. All these styles can trace their roots back to African rhythms. Mixed together into a spicy musical sauce, or salsa, this style of dance music rules nightclub dance floors in the United States, Latin America, and Europe.

Salsa evolved among primarily Puerto Rican, African American, South American, and Cuban musicians who played around New York City and Miami in the 1970s. They pioneered a sound that, like Cuban rumba and son, is led by the rhythms of the clave over which piano, a powerful horn section, bass, energetic percussion, and smooth vocals are added. The traditional Caribbean flavor of the music was given an up-tempo rock beat that audiences found irresistible.

In the 1980s, the style diversified when salsa romantica was created. This slow-dance music featured velvet-voiced singers who crooned romantic, and sometimes erotic, lyrics. During this era, the Cuban influence of salsa was reaffirmed when Cuban-born singer Gloria Estéfan became a major American star by mixing rock and pop with the salsa sound. Other stars, such as Ruben Blades, Willie Colón, Tito Puente, and Celia Cruz became international stars as a result of the salsa craze. In more recent years, singers such as Marc Anthony and Ricky Martin have blended salsa sensibilities with pop music to sell millions of records to dance-loving audiences.

ing big band beat to their sound with the addition of pianos, more horns, extra percussionists, and even flutes and violins. Cuban son remained popular throughout the world until 1959, when Communist dictator Fidel Castro took control of Cuba. This move prompted the U.S. government to institute an embargo against Cuba and restrict American travel to the island. Son music faded away, and some of Cuba's best son musicians struggled to survive on working menial jobs in Castro's Cuba.

Son music was reborn in the mid-1990s when slide guitar player and Los Angeles native Ry Cooder traveled to

The Cuban group Buena Vista Social Club introduced traditional son *music to a global audience.*

Cuba to explore the roots of son music. In 1996 Cooder and arranger Juan de Marcos Gonzalez recorded *Buena Vista Social Club*, featuring some of Cuba's best veteran son musicians, many of them well past the age of eighty. The album sold more than 2 million copies and reintroduced music fans to the style of Cuban music that first swept across the globe in the early decades of the twentieth century.

Carnival Sounds of Calypso

Calypso is a musical style from Trinidad that followed a similar path as Cuban son. The music emerged out of ancient African traditions in the nineteenth century, found popularity in New York and

Europe in the 1930s, and experienced faddish popularity in the 1950s. In calypso, however, unlike son and rumba, lyrics are as important as rhythms.

Calypso has had a powerful influence on the world of music since the twentieth century. The style, which features a strong, danceable beat with humorous, satirical, and often bawdy lyrics, has roots in African "praise songs" in which performers sang songs about the best or worst aspects of specific people. These performers were the news reporters of previous centuries, walking from house to house singing derogatory songs about people who had committed various wrongs. Those accused could not answer directly but were free to sing songs in their own defense.

Buena Vista Social Club

In 1996 guitarist Ry Cooder recorded veteran son musicians for the album and the movie Buena Vista Social Club. *The album, which sold more than 2 million copies and won a Grammy Award, is described by Chris Nickson in* The NPR Curious Listener's Guide to World Music:

Most of [the musicians on *Buena Vista Social Club*] had ended their careers, and were living in obscurity when the opportunity came knocking. The late Compay Segundo, now in his nineties, proved to be a charismatic figure, but all the major figures involved with the record had their own magic. Ibrahim Ferrer, who'd been supplementing his pension by shining shoes and selling lottery tickets, proved to be a remarkable voice and a quick study. Omara Portuondo, who'd been a star in the 1950s, had lost very little of her voice, and now-deceased Ruben Gonzalez, who'd hardly touched a piano in years, quickly found his touch, in spite of arthritis. In fact, he more than found his touch; once sessions were finished, the crew took two more days to record a solo album for Gonzalez. It wasn't long before both Ferrer and Portuondo were also recording their own albums, while Segundo signed a contract and recorded for another label. *Buena Vista Social Club* was the kind of phenomenon no one could have predicted. The music was blatantly nostalgic, but it somehow struck a chord around the world, selling several million copies. The troupe toured, and Wim Wenders's [1999 movie of the same name] was also a hit with audiences. In the wake of all this came the Cuban explosion. . . . Suddenly, record store shelves were filled with products from Cuba.

In Trinidad, this ancient custom became entangled with the Catholic tradition called carnival, brought to the island by Spanish and French colonial planters. Similar to the annual Mardi Gras festival held in New Orleans, carnival is a masquerade ball and parade celebrated with spirited drinking, dancing, and singing before the onset of Lent, a forty-day period of fasting and penance leading up to Easter.

In the wild carnival atmosphere, black artists could sing songs criticizing government figures while wearing

Soca Sounds

In the 1970s, a new brand of Trinidad music, called soca, melded calypso with music of the island's Indian immigrants. The invention of the style by calypso performer Lord Shorty is detailed on the "CaribPlanet" Web site:

Soca is a modern form of calypso with an up-tempo beat. . . . Soca music originated as a fusion of calypso with Indian rhythms, thus combining the musical traditions to the two major ethnic groups of Trinidad and Tobago. . . . Garfield Blackman would become the creator of soca. Blackman began singing calypso at the tender age of seven. Performing under the name Lord Shorty, he rose to fame in 1963 with his recording of "Cloak and Dagger." The name Lord Shorty is a paradoxical reference to his imposing height of 6-ft 4-inches.

Talk that calypso was dying, and reggae was the new thing, prompted Lord Shorty to . . . combine Indian rhythm instruments (particularly the [drums] dholak, tabla and [the percussion instrument] dhantal) with traditional calypso music. The result was a new energetic musical hybrid called soca. In 1973, Lord Shorty introduced soca to the world with his hit song "Ïndrani." The release of his 1974 album *Endless Vibrations* prompted dozens of musicians to adopt the new soca style.

Lord Shorty initially referred to his musical hybrid as "solka" representing the true "soul of calypso." . . . The name was later changed to "soca" by a music journalist. . . .

Soca has continued to grow and evolve, giving rise to offshoots such as ragga [digital reggae] soca and the increasingly popular chutney [Indian-influenced] soca. Today soca is the definitive indigenous musical form associated with the Eastern Caribbean.

Revelers dance to soca music in Trinidad.

masks and costumes to hide their identity. By the early twentieth century, this form of song had evolved into calypso. During this era, calypso songs acted as a cable TV news service might today. Lyrics of calypso songs, especially those concerning political corruption, were discussed and debated by politicians and average citizens. This grassroots musical commentary was considered the most accurate news source by islanders, but often incited the ire of government officials who ordered police officials to analyze and censor certain songs.

In the 1930s, Trinidad's major calypso stars had gained the notice of audiences the world over, and singers such as Attila the Hun, Roaring Lion, Lord Invader, and Lord Kitchener began selling records internationally. Kitchener remained a popular calypso star for decades, producing hit records until his death in 2001.

In the United States, the most renowned calypso hit was "Banana Boat Song" by Harry Belafonte. This song, which is still heard on oldies-format radio stations, was the first calypso record to sell over 1 million copies.

Jamaica International

As an island ruled by Great Britain, Trinidad attracted people from British colonies in the Caribbean, especially Jamaica. By the 1920s, Trinidad calypso was exerting a powerful influence on Jamaican musicians, who played music with hand drums, rattles, fifes, and banjos while singing often witty songs featuring topical and narrative commentary. This form, called *mento,* was popular among the rural poor in the Jamaican countryside.

By the 1950s, mento was the national music of Jamaica, often sung to tourists who came to the island on cruise ships. Sometimes called Jamaican calypso, mento bands capitalized on the Trinidad fad by naming their bands Lord Messam and His Calypsonians, Count Lasher's Calypso Quintet, and Reynold's Calypso Clippers. The lyrics of these rhythmic songs were often humorous accounts of everyday life in the poor neighborhoods of Kingston, along with tales of romance.

While mento remained a local phenomenon, Jamaican music went international in the 1960s when some of the island's finest musicians invented a new sound called ska. This music blended mento, rhythm and blues, faster "jump" blues, and boogie with a new and exciting beat. While boogie has a driving 4/4 rhythm, in which every beat is emphasized, in ska guitar players highlighted single chops, or strums on the offbeat. This danceable, syncopated music was played at a rapid, galloping tempo, with drum rolls pushing the rhythm and horn players blowing melodic jazz phrases.

The most popular ska group in Jamaica was the Skatalites, who scored hit after hit on the island. However, ska did not gain international attention until vocalist Millie Small scored a hit with the song "My Boy Lollipop." Although the

Jamaican musician Bob Marley popularized reggae music in the 1960s.

ska fad ended after several months in the United States and after a few years in Jamaica, the musical style remained popular in Great Britain and was revived in the late 1970s and early 1980s by the English bands the Specials, Madness, and the Beat. In the 1990s, it was once again revived on the other side of the Atlantic, in a different form, by American group No Doubt.

Reggae International

If ska had been the last word in Jamaican music, the island might have remained a footnote in music history.

However, the invention of reggae in the late 1960s made Jamaica a musical powerhouse and changed music history forever. Reggae was born in the late 1960s in the recording studios of Jamaica's capital city of Kingston, when producers were looking for a new beat to capture the attention of the island's discerning music fans. The evolution started with a style called rocksteady, a slow, rhythmic music in which the drummer hit the deep-toned bass drum or floor tom once, on the third beat of every measure. Rocksteady also featured a prominent bass line playing a catchy melody. This style, highlighting bass and drums, was melded with the old-fashioned mento shuffle and a new rhythm, dubbed reggae, was born. Lyrically, reggae also featured traces of calypso, with verses often expressing the viewpoint common to those who had long fought repression and the colonial system imposed on them by outsiders.

Although he did not make the first reggae record, Bob Marley was the first to take the music to an international audience. Working with Peter Tosh and Bunny Wailer in the group the Wailers, Marley recorded *Catch a Fire*, a 1973 album produced specifically to take the appeal of reggae to white college students in the United States. While the album did not catch on as expected, Marley was recognized by an international array of critics and fans in 1975 when English rock star Eric Clapton covered his song "I Shot the Sheriff."

In the following years, Marley released the albums *Natty Dread, Live!* and *Rastaman Vibration.* These records were extremely influential, as Mikal Gilmore attests in an authoritative profile on Marley in *Rolling Stone:*

> Like the milestone albums of the Beatles, Bob Dylan, Jimi Hendrix, the Rolling Stones, Marvin Gaye and Sly Stone, these were records that created new sonic ground and changed how we would hear music. They were also albums that announced Marley as a pre-eminent musical figure.[45]

Although Marley died in 1981, reggae lives on, changing and growing with each new generation. The reggae beat can be heard in Afropop, rock and roll, and other musical styles from Latin America, Asia, Africa, and elsewhere. In Jamaica, the music evolved into *ragga*—a digital style with reggae rhythms—and dub, reggae with rap lyrics. As the most enduring and popular sound from the region, reggae seems unstoppable. For music fans, it is but one of the many fine ingredients that make up the influential musical potpourri that has emerged from the Caribbean.

Chapter Seven

Music of Latin America

It is little wonder that the diverse nations of Latin America have produced a wide array of unique music over the years. In more than twenty nations covering an area that stretches from northern Mexico through Central and South America, the people in this expansive region speak Spanish, Portuguese, French, and dozens of in-digenous languages and local dialects. They live in places as diverse as the towering Andes mountains, the rain forests of Brazil, the barren plains of the Mexican desert, and the stunning seacoast of Chile. Their societies have absorbed influences from numerous cultures including indigenous Indian, Spanish, Portuguese, African, West

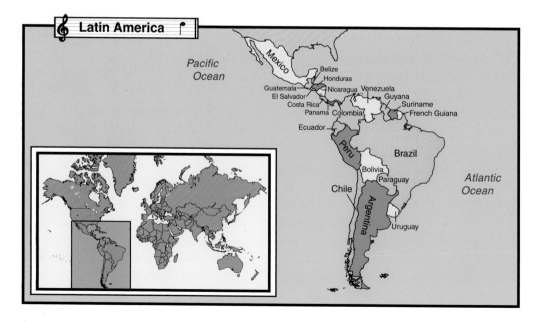

Latin America

Pacific Ocean

Mexico

Belize
Honduras
Guatemala — Nicaragua Venezuela
El Salvador — Guyana
Costa Rica — Suriname
Panama Colombia — French Guiana
Ecuador —

Peru

Brazil

Bolivia
Paraguay

Chile

Argentina

Atlantic Ocean

Uruguay

Indian, and American. With this multicultural background, it is not unusual to hear a Latin American band using African drums and Indian flutes while singing Spanish lyrics mixed with native dialect.

As the population of Latin America continues to grow, the countries south of the U.S. border are playing an important role in the world music market. Radio and Internet stations dedicated to Latin music are increasing, and some artists have achieved superstardom on an international scale.

Indigenous Music Today

Archaeologists believe that the ancient peoples of west-central Mexico were producing musical instruments around 200 B.C. Decorative clay flutes with finger holes have been found alongside rattles, scrapers, bone strikers, conch shells, drums, and other instruments. Around that time, high in the Peruvian Andes, Incan musicians were playing ceramic ten-tube panpipes, or *siku.* The indigenous musical traditions of these people were not confined to Peru, however; similar instruments have been found in the Andes chain in Chile, Venezuela, and elsewhere.

Today, the musical roots of the ancient Andes are still heard among the Quechua people of Peru, Ecuador, and Bolivia. Like many other forms of Latin American music, the traditional native songs in these areas are diverse and unique. Neighboring villages may produce music that varies in the ways instruments are tuned, the methods the

A boy plays the traditional panpipes in Bolivia's Altiplano region.

songs are sung, and even the five-, six-, or seven-note scales that are used. In addition, these villagers have adapted various sounds of European origin and blended them with their indigenous traditions.

The ancient sounds of panpipes play a central role in much of the indigenous music of the Andes. Made from ceramics, bamboo, or wood, these pipes are frequently played in pairs. Attached to one another by a cord, one pipe of the pair has half the notes needed to play a melody, while the other pipe has the remaining notes. These must be played by two musicians who alternate notes to play a complete melody. As

Jan Fairley writes in *World Music, Volume 2:* "While symbolically this demonstrates the reciprocity within the community, practically it enables players to play for a long time without getting too 'high' from the dizziness caused by over-breathing."[46]

Since the sixteenth century, duo and single panpipes have been played at weddings, dances, and other festivities by bands with up to fifty members. This boisterous sound is backed by musicians playing large, deep-toned drums called *bombos*.

Most people outside of the Andes never hear fifty-member panpipe bands. However, smaller bands of Andean musicians are commonly seen entertaining in tourist towns and on college campuses in Europe, Canada, Japan, and the United States. These folk bands, dressed in ponchos and other traditional garb, play panpipes, *bombos, charangos* (a ten-string guitarlike instrument), guitars, and notched-end flutes called *quenas*. This phenomenon began in 1970 after the best-selling American musical duo Simon and Garfunkel introduced Andean music to the world by recording a modern version of the traditional song "El Condor Pasa." In the years that followed, Andean "poncho bands" have played for tips in town squares from Prague to Provincetown, entertaining passersby with traditional tunes.

Tales of Revolutions and Gangsters

Like the Andean nations, Mexico has a long musical history heavily influenced by Spanish culture. The traditional folk music of Mexico, *corrido*, has roots in long epic ballads popular in Spain in the eighteenth century. As with the African griot and Trinidad calypso traditions, corrido folk ballads often provide details of notable events and have served as a primary method of spreading news among an often isolated populace. For example, when the Mexican Revolution began in 1910, corrido was used to convey the heroic deeds of revolutionaries such as Emiliano Zapata as well as tragic outcomes of battles. The lyrical excerpt from "Valentín de la Sierra" is an example of the latter:

> I'm going to sing a corrido
>
> about a friend from my land.
>
> He was called Valentín
>
> and he was shot and hung in the sierra.
>
> I don't want to recall
>
> it was a winter afternoon when
>
> From bad luck
>
> Valentín fell into the hands of government forces.[47]

Corrido is usually played with accordions, guitars, and various percussion instruments in a waltz beat, that is, 3/4 time. The songs most often follow a fixed format. The song begins with a salutation from the singer and a short prologue to the story. It continues with the story itself. The moral of the story follows and then a farewell from the vocalist.

Norteño *musicians, such as these two in Guanajuato, Mexico, sing songs about controversial subjects such as narcotics traffickers.*

In recent years, the corrido has evolved in northern Mexico into *norteño* music and its antigovernment lyrics have changed to fit the times. Modern norteño singers tell stories about the hardships of oppressed workers and the deeds of political agitators. The most controversial songs, called *narcocorrido*, glorify the violent deeds of drug growers, gangsters, and narcotics traffickers. While often criticized in the press, norteño music remains popular among Mexican youth much the same way that gansta rap appeals to many in the United States.

Norteño is also the favorite music of many undocumented immigrants who try to illegally cross the border into the United States. The lyrics to the popular "Cruce el Rio Grande" tells the tale of one unfortunate immigrant:

I crossed the Rio Grande

Swimming, not giving a damn

The Border Patrol threw me back

I disguised myself as a gringo

And tinted my hair blonde

But since I don't know English

Back I go again[48]

Powerful New Song

The corrido of Mexico has found another form, called *nueva canción*, or "new music," in nations such as Chile, Argentina, and Uruguay, where protests, revolutions, and violent political upheavals have been common throughout the twentieth century. Songwriters of the nueva canción style compose lyrics critical of repressive governments and the political turmoil that roils their nations. This development is described by John M. Schechter in *Worlds of Music:*

> *Nueva Canción* is a song movement that stands up for one's own culture, for one's own people, in the face of oppression by a totalitarian government or in the face of "cultural imperialism" from abroad, notably the United States and Europe. . . . *Nueva Canción* artists seek to reinvoke and revalidate traditional lifeways of forgotten persons or people. These musicians express their social consciousness. They speak out in a clear voice against conditions of oppression, advocating social change.[49]

These popular ballads spread news about the misdeeds of dictators and the actions of protesters. However, only the bravest musicians risk their lives by criticizing violently repressive government officials who may censor, ban, exile, jail, torture, and kill musicians who oppose their policies. Chilean singer and songwriter Victor Jara is one of many such victims. In 1970 a political revolution swept through Chile as Socialist politician Salvador Allende was elected president with the help of Jara's supportive nueva canción songs. When Allende was overthrown by military dictator Augusto Pinochet in September 1973, Jara

Chilean singer and songwriter Victor Jara was executed in 1973. Here, his widow participates in a ceremony held in his honor.

Victor Jara

Victor Jara is considered a musical hero by many because the lyrics of his nueva canción, or "new song," challenged the repressive politicians who used torture and murder to control Chile in the 1960s and 1970s. When military dictator Augusto Pinochet took control of Chile in 1973, Jara was arrested and held at Chile Stadium, a soccer stadium in Santiago, with five thousand other prisoners. Later Jara was taken to jail, where he wrote the words to the song "Chile Stadium." The lyrics were smuggled out of the prison before the singer was again taken to the stadium, where his hands were broken and burned while his torturers taunted him to play his guitar. Jara was later machine-gunned to death. His lyrics to "Chile Stadium," below, are from the "Latin American Music" Web page.

"Chile Stadium"

There are five thousand of us here

in this little part of the city.

We are five thousand.

I wonder how many we are in all

in the cities and in the whole country? Here alone

are ten thousand hands which plant seeds

and make the factories run:

How much humanity

exposed to hunger, cold, panic, pain,

moral pressures, terror and insanity?

What horror the face of fascism creates!

How hard it is to sing

when I must sing of horror.

Horror which I am living.

Horror which I am dying.

To see myself among so much horror

and so many moments of infinity

in which silence and screams

are the end of my song.

What I see I have never seen.

What I have felt and what I feel

will give birth to the moment. . . .

was publicly tortured and murdered in a Santiago soccer stadium, where he had previously given a concert for Allende.

As part of Pinochet's violent policies, other musicians also fell victim. Dale A. Olsen explains in *The Garland*

Handbook of Latin American Music: "Because panpipes, notch flutes, and [*charangos*] were featured in the protest movement . . . Pinochet made their playing unlawful."[50] This led to the arrest and disappearance of hundreds of musicians who played the traditional instruments.

In further retaliation, nueva canción was banned from airwaves and cassettes of the music were destroyed. Concerts were prohibited and radio stations were forbidden from playing the music. Although nueva canción was forced underground, it remained a vital force of news and commentary until Pinochet was removed from office in 1990. The style was also heard in other repressive Latin American countries such as Nicaragua and Cuba.

In the years after Jara's death, his songs continue to be held in high esteem and have been recorded by superstars such as Jackson Browne, Peter Gabriel, Bruce Springsteen, and Sting. And in nations where nueva canción helped keep hope alive for millions, the old songs from the sixties and seventies are considered by some to be nearly as important as national anthems.

Tango in Argentina

The often-tragic music of nueva canción is but one of the hundreds of genres that have developed in the Latin American world. The region has also produced a profusion of dance hall musical styles, such as the tango, the samba, and the bossa nova, that have inspired countless dancers the world over. However, even these popular sounds have roots in South America's often-sorrowful history of slavery and poverty.

The tango is a good example of a musical genre and related dance that spread from the most downtrodden elements of Argentinean culture to international high society. The roots of the tango can be traced to the early twentieth century when gangsters, petty criminals, and impoverished laborers in Buenos Aires, Argentina, patronized seedy barrooms. These disreputable nightclubs had few women customers so men danced with one another. The tango developed as a way for aggressive men to compete in a mock battle. Eventually the tango moved to places where women could be found, mainly brothels where it is said that prostitutes chose their clients by their tango skills.

At the time, dancers in polite society maintained a respectable distance of several inches from one another while circling the dance floor. The tango, by contrast, was considered scandalous and immoral because couples danced cheek-to-cheek and exchanged caresses with their chests pressed together and their legs intertwined.

The music of the tango was played on inexpensive instruments available to the poor, including flute, guitar, violin, and a concertina-like instrument called a *bandoneón*. In later years, tango bands grew in size to include the double bass, piano, and several violins and *bandoneónes*. Tango musicians put together sounds from a broad range of influences that included Spanish flamenco, Italian popular song, Cuban dance styles, African drum music, European polkas, and even folk songs played by Argentinean gauchos or cowboys.

Although tango was shunned by most in Buenos Aires society, an upper-class Argentinean writer, Ricardo Güiraldes, was a fan of the music and the dance. In 1911 he wrote "Tango," a poem that compared the dance to an "all-absorbing love of a tyrant, jealously guarding his dominion, over women who have surrendered submissively, like obedient beasts."[51] Ironically, this shocking verse helped end resistance to the tango among Argentina's elite. The following year, Güiraldes gave a tango demonstration to members of Paris's high society, and within months the tango craze swept through the salons and ballrooms of upper-class Europe. In the 1920s, the tango fad became firmly entrenched in the United States when America's

The tango is an Argentinean musical genre that has become popular throughout the world.

biggest movie star, Rudolph Valentino, performed the dance in the 1926 film *The Four Horsemen of the Apocalypse.*

Tango music followed the popularity of the dance during the golden age of tango from 1925 to 1945. No longer the domain of unschooled barroom players, tango was performed by the best musicians in the business. During this golden age, Argentinean bandleader Roberto Firpo and singer Carlos Gardel helped make tango music an international success.

The widespread popularity of tango began to wane when rock and roll came to dominate the airwaves in the 1950s. However, the music with the irresistible dance rhythm did not fade away. In the 1960s, bandoneón player Astor Piazzolla pioneered the *nuevo,* or "new," tango by experimenting with unusual chord patterns, rhythms, and harmonies. In the 1970s, Argentinean rockers combined the old music with electric guitars and synthesizers to produce *tango rockéro,* or "tango rock." In more recent times, musicians have continued to update the sound with a genre labeled neo-tango, electro tango, or tango fusion. The music still has the tango beat, but it is augmented with complex polyrhythms, digital instruments, and intricate melodies.

In Paris, the Gotan Project is playing tango with electronic samples, beats, and sounds superimposed on the tango rhythm. Meanwhile, the rise in popularity of salsa and other dance styles has once again made traditional tango music a hot commodity among dance fans. With a rhythm infused with the colorful history of Argentinean gangsters, Hollywood movie stars, and Parisian high society, tango remains a musical style with appeal to many segments of society.

Samba Sounds from Brazil

Argentina is not the only South American country closely associated with a dance style. In Brazil, the samba has come to represent the national identity of a country steeped in music. And the samba, like the tango, developed among the lowest classes of society.

Brazil has the largest black population of any nation outside Africa, and most black Brazilians are descendents of slaves. Some of these slaves were taught to play European instruments by the Portuguese planters who colonized Brazil. In 1748 French priest René de la Blanchardière wrote: "Violins are heard in most of the houses: every master is careful to have his Negroes taught to play that instrument. There are many guitars; several trumpets are to be heard, too, which produce a rather pleasant harmony."[52] In addition, slaves were taught to play clarinet, piano, and flute.

When not performing for the plantation owners, slaves used their European instruments to play their own African-influenced music. They were joined by percussionists who played rattles, drums, and homemade rhythm instruments. This music was played for dancers, whose movements were described by Louis-François de Tollenare in 1817:

The Songs of Brazilian Workers

Music has long been a part of everyday life in Brazil. In the nineteenth century, singing helped ease the burden of slaves who accompanied themselves on percussion instruments as they carried heavy loads on their heads. In 1851 American missionary Charles Samuel Stewart described the songs he heard from work gangs and others on the streets of Rio de Janeiro. His words are reprinted in Rhythms of Resistance *by Peter Fryer:*

[T]he] first sight which arrests the eyes of the stranger on landing in Rio is the number, varied employments, and garb of the negroes. The first and chief human sounds that reach his ears are also from this class. Their cries through the streets vary with the pursuits they follow. That of the vegetable and fruit venders is monotonous and singular; but also varied, that each kind of vegetable and fruit seems to have its own song. The coffee-carriers, moving in gangs, have a tune of their own to which they keep time, in an Indian-like lope, with a bag of one hundred and sixty pounds' weight, poised on their heads. The bearers of furniture form a regular choir. One or two, with rattles of tin in their hands, resembling the [spout] of a watering-pot, perforated with holes and filled with shot, lead the way in a style truly African. To this is allied, with full strength of lungs, a kind of travelling chant, in which at times all join in chorus. It is full and sonorous, and rendered pleasant, if from no other cause, by the satisfaction from it visible, in the shining and sweating faces of the poor blacks.

It was a lively and extraordinary shaking of all the body's principle muscles, and a very indecent movement of hips and buttocks. . . . the dancers vie with each other as to who can keep it going the longest, and the people's applause rewards those whose muscles are most sturdy and, above all, most mobile.[53]

This type of dance, known as the *Jundú*, evolved in the twentieth century into the samba in the Rio de Janeiro barrio known as Little Africa. The former slaves who settled in the neighborhood perfected the samba to perform at Carnaval, the wild spring festival similar to Mardi Gras during which thousands of costumed celebrants take to the streets to dance, drink, and parade in the days before Lent. Although Carnaval is celebrated in many Catholic countries, the Brazilian version is most intense, as David Cleary writes in *World Music, Volume 2:* "In Brazil, somehow, Carnaval, got out of control. . . . [It] goes further—in every sense—than anywhere else. From the Friday [before Carnaval] the country shuts down for five days . . . practically the whole population gets down to the most serious partying in the world."[54]

Carnaval revolves around the shuffling, rhythmic samba music played by musicians using tooth-rattling samba drums, sizzling percussion, and even shrill coaches' whistles. The music is described by Morales:

The numbers of drummers involved in a large Brazilian samba batería (group of drummers) are staggering. During a typical winter carnaval, hundreds of sambistas [samba players] are playing a wide variety of drums, most of which have rough equivalents in

Carnaval celebrations in Rio de Janeiro revolve around the sounds of rhythmic Brazilian samba music.

various other Latin American traditions, but some of which are unique to Brazil. Brazil has more varieties of percussion instruments than any other country in the Western Hemisphere. Surdos are very much like Dominican or Venezuelan tamboras [small drums played with sticks], the caixa is similar to snare drums, the agogô is like the salsa cowbell, the pandeira like the Puerto Rican pandareta (a tambourine-like instrument played during Christmas celebrations). The samba is a call to wild, mass movement, an orgy of percussion.[55]

Samba might have remained a local phenomenon were it not for singer and actress Carmen Miranda, known as the Brazilian Bombshell. Miranda, who appeared wearing her now-iconic fruit headdress, introduced the world to the driving rhythms, intricate melodies, and lyrical poetry of samba in several Hollywood movies in the early 1940s.

Unlike the tango, the samba remained a vital force in Brazil, and its popularity never faded. In the 1960s, the hot samba beat was slowed by guitarist João Gilberto, who added elements of jazz to create the cool, sophisticated sounds of bossa nova, literally "new beat." This music was epitomized in the sixties song "The Girl From Ipanema" —the biggest international hit to ever emerge from Brazil—by Gilberto's wife, Astrud. The bossa nova beat was enthusiastically adopted by American jazz artists such as Stan Getz, Dizzy Gillespie, and Herbie Mann.

In the early seventies, the Brazilian beat continued to flourish. Credit may be given to percussionist Airto Moreira, who popularized the use of traditional drums, congas, rattles, and a wide assortment of percussion instruments in rock and jazz music. Moreira brought the Brazilian sound to American audiences while jamming with his wife, jazz vocalist Flora Purim; trumpeter Miles Davis; pianist Herbie Hancock; and the rock band the Grateful Dead.

In the 1990s, samba, like other traditional styles, was melded with rock, rap, electronic dance, and other genres by those hoping to reach a younger audience. Funk, reggae, soul, and rhythm and blues (R & B) have also been brought into the Brazilian musical mix.

At the beginning of a new millennium, as the population of Latin America approaches 800 million, Brazil, Mexico, Argentina, and other nations continue to influence musical styles worldwide. With roots in African, indigenous, and European cultures, the music of Latin America will continue to inspire.

Chapter Eight

World Music of the United States

The United States is recognized the world over for having pioneered the most popular—and profitable—musical genres in history, including blues, jazz, ragtime, R & B, and rock and roll. Like music from Latin America, the Caribbean, and elsewhere, these styles were invented by black musicians who combined elements of African and European music to create new sounds.

While rock, jazz, and blues are not considered world music, American musicians have produced lesser known sounds that are now placed in that category. Native American, Cajun, zydeco, Tex-Mex, and Hawaiian music, like other styles in the world music

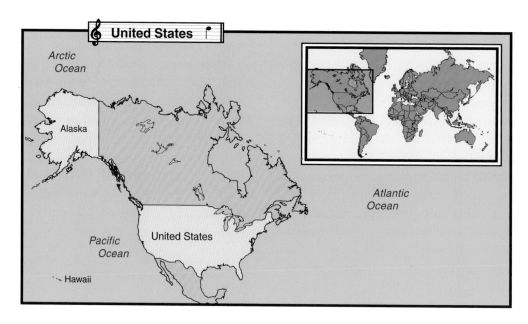

The music made by Native Americans, such as these Navajo drummers of the early 1900s, is as diverse as the many different Indian tribes.

genre, bring together indigenous roots music with modern instruments and updated lyrics. The music is also shaped by the ethnic identities of the musicians.

Music from the First Americans

Indians, the first Americans, have lived in what is now the United States for at least thirteen thousand years, so their music is the original sound of America. However, the music of the 3 million Native Americans living in the United States and Canada is as diverse as their varied tribal heritage. From the eastern Atlantic shores through the plains, mountains, deserts, and forests of the West, each of the continent's thousands of Indian tribes developed its own specific style of music.

While extremely varied, traditional Native American music shared some basic similarities. Most songs were ceremonial in nature, and each tribe created a repertoire of music performed for important events such as healing, hunting, celebration, war, birth, and death. Other songs were concerned with deities that represented natural elements such as the sun, rain, corn, trees, and countless animals. According to traditional beliefs, songs such as "Sun Dance," "Deer Dance," and "Corn Dance" were taught to Native Americans by the gods through visions and dreams.

Traditional Native American music, still performed today, uses a chorus of singers, drummers, and percussionists. Many of the ancient songs are performed at Indian intertribal gatherings called powwows. However, a great body of ceremonial music remains sacred and is rarely, if ever, played for the general public.

Modern Indian music, however, is much more than healing dances, honor

Buffy Sainte-Marie, a Cree Indian, performed songs protesting the Vietnam War and the taking of Indian lands.

chants, and songs to the sunrise. Since the 1960s, Native American performers have picked up modern band instruments such as guitars, drums, saxophones, and accordions. Like musicians who have had to deal with racism and government oppression in Latin America, Africa, and elsewhere, these players produced music with a distinctive message. In 1969 Lakota activist, musician, and actor Floyd Red Crow Westerman, born in South Dakota, became a prominent proponent of Indian views. Accompanying himself on guitar, Westerman sings about his often-bitter experiences with government boarding schools, Indian reservations, and the harsh treatment of native people. On the title track of the 1969 album *Custer Died for Your Sins*, Westerman explains why General George Armstrong Custer and his army deserved to be slaughtered at Little Bighorn in Montana in 1876:

> For the lies that were spoken
>
> For the blood that we have spilled
>
> For the treaties that were broken
>
> For the leaders you have stilled
>
> Custer died for your sins[56]

Westerman was one of several singers expressing the Indian point of view. Canadian-born Buffy Sainte-Marie, a Cree who grew up in Massachusetts, toured colleges, reservations, and concert halls playing her song "Universal Soldier," which became an anthem of the peace movement in the late sixties. Sainte-Marie's song "Now That the Buffalo's Gone" poetically protests the taking of Indian lands by white Americans. Sainte-Marie's music, like that of Westerman's, found an international audience in Europe, Asia, South America, and elsewhere. While their music was topical to Native Americans, many felt it expressed the emotions, hopes, and dreams for justice held by other ill-treated peoples throughout the world.

In the 1970s, a younger generation of Indian musicians played a heavier brand of rock music with updated themes concerning environmental degradation, political disillusionment, and the need for greater recognition in mainstream society. The group XIT, formed in the early seventies, was a rock band with albums such as *Plight of the Redman* and *Without Reservation* that put a hard-charging, unflinching rock-and-roll edge on songs dealing with Indian issues.

A New Age of Native American Music

In the 1990s, singer and songwriter Keith Secola, an Anishinabe from northern Minnesota, added traditional elements, such as powwow-style drumming and group singing, to rock music to produce a modern hybrid of Indian music. Secola also often reflects modern Native American concerns in a humorous context. The lyrics to his song "NDN [Indian] Cars," about the broken-down jalopies often seen on reservations, provide a good example:

My car is dented
the radiator steams

Headlights don't work
radio can scream

Got a sticker says "Indian Power"
on my bumper

Holds my car together

We're on a circuit of an Indian
dream. . . .

Flying down the highway
riding in r NDN cars[57]

Native American music has gone beyond rock and roll and some styles have been discovered by lovers of new age music. The 1980s saw the revival of traditional wooden flute music, led by Navajo-Ute R. Carlos Nakai. His 1983 album, *Canyons*, which sold nearly 3 million copies, is filled with hauntingly beautiful songs that evoke the mystery and splendor of the pristine natural world. On later albums, Nakai blends his flute with sounds of nature and sweeping digital synthesizers to produce new age records that have sold millions throughout the world. With four Grammy nominations and dozens of awards for his work, Nakai appeals to fans of world music, new age, and Native American music alike.

The group Walela also brings a new age feel to Native American sounds on their albums *Walela* and *Unbearable Love*. While putting a lyrical spin on Indian history and culture, the group's three vocalists, Rita Coolidge, her sister Priscilla Coolidge, and Priscilla's daughter Laura Satterfield, blend stunning gospel-tinged harmonies with melodies reminiscent of ancient times.

Members of Walela also provide vocals on albums by Robbie Robertson, a half-Mohawk songwriter and guitarist. Robertson first achieved fame in the mid-1960s playing lead guitar for Bob Dylan. In the 1970s, he played and wrote songs, such as "The Night They Drove Old Dixie Down," with the popular rock group the Band. In the 1990s, Robertson returned to his Mohawk roots with an album titled *Music for Native Americans*, recorded with the Red Road Ensemble, a Native American group. With songs such as "Heartbeat Drum Song" and "Golden Feather," Robertson combined the intricate textures of Native American song, modern rock, and electronic programming.

Robertson's 1998 album, *Contact from the Underworld of Redboy*, is even more focused on the musician's Mohawk heritage, mixing elements of Native American music with ultramodern sounds. The critically acclaimed album was nominated for two Grammy Awards in the world music category. Speaking about his motivation for making *Contact from the Underworld of Redboy*, Robertson had this to say:

> When I was making this record . . . it struck me that this musicality from the Native community of North America has always lived in this very secretive, private, oppressed, and sometimes illegal place. . . . Native music has lived underground for so long, and now it's time to step forward. It's time to do what we can just to share this with people.[58]

Cajuns Let the Good Times Roll

While Native American music has roots in nearly every part of North America, one of the most popular regional styles in the United States originated in the South. However, the roots of Cajun music, associated with Louisiana, can be traced to the freezing maritime province of present-day Nova Scotia, Canada.

In the eighteenth century, thousands of French people lived in Nova Scotia, an area they called Acadia. They were forced from their homes in 1755 by British soldiers. Some went back to France, but about three thousand eventually made their way to Louisiana, which was then governed by France. The Acadians settled in southwest Louisiana, around Lafayette. Their neighbors were French-speaking blacks from the Caribbean and whites from Spain, Germany, and the United States. The Acadians kept their culture intact and played their traditional music. By the 1860s, the term *Acadians* had shortened to *Cajuns*.

This exiled group of impoverished Cajuns labored in the fields from sunrise to sunset. At night, families gathered to sing long, unaccompanied songs called *complaintes* about life in previous centuries. These were sung

Hawaiian Slack Key Guitar

In the early twentieth century, the unique music of Hawaii began to influence sounds on the American mainland as more Hawaiian records were sold in the United States than any other type. Hawaii's early contribution to world music was driven by the slide, or slack key, guitar, which was later adopted by country and western swing musicians. Guitarist and Hawaiian music historian Keola Beamer describes the development of the sound on the Web site "A Brief History of Slack Key Guitar":

[H]awaiian slack key guitar (ki ho'alu) is truly one of the great acoustic guitar traditions in the world. Ki ho'alu, which literally means "loosen the key," is the Hawaiian language name for the solo finger-picked style unique to Hawai'i. In this tradition, the strings (or "keys") are "slacked" to produce many different tunings. . . . Each tuning produces a lingering sound behind the melody and has a characteristic resonance and fingering.

Many Hawaiian songs and slack key guitar pieces reflect themes like stories of the past and present and people's lives. But it is the tropical surroundings of Hawai'i, with its oceans, volcanoes and mountains, waterfalls, forests, plants and animals, that provide the deepest source of inspiration for Hawaiian music. . . . Slack key guitar music is sweet and soulful, and it is said that slack key is drawn from the heart and soul out through the fingers of each player. . . .

Because Hawai'i is one of the crossroads of the world, its music has always had many influences: Latin music from Mexico, Spain and Portugal; Polynesian music, especially from Samoa and Tahiti; European music and music from the Mainland, including jazz, country & western, folk and pop. All have been absorbed by Hawaiians, and they have enriched it with their mana (soul).

The slack key guitar was introduced by traditional Hawaiian groups such as this.

with songs about love, drinking, dancing, and ballads about historic wars and tragedy.

On weekends, Cajuns believed it was time to *laissez les bon temps rouler*, or "let the good times roll," a phrase closely associated with Cajun music today. To let the good times roll, people packed into dances in barns, living rooms, and taverns. Plenty of alcohol was consumed as people gathered to dance jigs, reels, the energetic two-step, and waltzes in 3/4 time. These boisterous dances had the ironic name *fais do do*, or "make sleep" in French, because it was said that the children had to be put to bed before the adults could start having fun.

Musicians at these noisy gatherings were limited to playing the loudest instruments, primarily a few fiddles, with a shrill vocalist singing French lyrics above the din. Eventually a raucous rhythm instrument was added, an iron triangle played with a metal rod. By the 1850s, German immigrants had introduced the accordion to the region, and this soon made its appearance at Cajun dances, primarily because it too was very loud. The addition of the accordion changed Cajun music. While violins could play complex melodies in many keys, the ten-button chromatic accordions had a very limited range. This meant accordionists could play only two or three chord changes, as in the structure of basic blues and rock music.

Cajun music was little known outside Louisiana until 1928 when accordionist Joe Falcon and his wife, guitarist and vocalist Cleoma Breaux Falcon, recorded a tuneful two-step, "Alons à Lafayette," for the Columbia

Cajun music was developed by French immigrants in Louisiana. In this 1977 photo, accordionist Nathan Abshire performs at the Cajun Music Festival.

label. Soon after, Cleoma and her brothers recorded another song, "Ma Blonde Est Partie," now known as "Jolie Blonde." Both songs sold well throughout the United States and are now much-performed Cajun classics.

By the time the Falcons made their records, Cajun musicians had added guitars and an unusual rhythm instrument, the washboard. This implement had a rough glass surface that was used for scrubbing clothes but also made for an irresistible rhythm track when scraped with metal spoons or bottle openers.

Despite the national success of several Cajun records, Cajun culture was under assault in Louisiana. French was banned in public schools in 1916, and many young Cajuns were moving away and becoming Americanized. By the early sixties, Cajun culture was virtually extinct. However, over the years, a small group of folklorists and musical scholars had remained interested in the music. In 1964 these musical historians traveled to Louisiana to scour the countryside for Cajun acts to book at the prestigious Newport Folk Festival in Rhode Island.

They found a school bus driver and fiddler, Dewey Balfa, and his fiddling farmer brother, Will Balfa, who still played the traditional songs on weekends with a guitarist and accordionist. Although the men had never left south Louisiana, they soon found themselves playing classic Cajun hits to seventeen thousand people who repeatedly gave them standing ovations.

This prompted the Balfa Brothers, who had never played to more than a few dozen people in a local bar, to quit their jobs and begin playing full time. Soon they were touring U.S. colleges, playing music, and presenting lectures and workshops about Cajun culture and music. Before his death in 1992, Dewey Balfa was responsible for making Cajun music part of Louisiana school curriculum and was considered a full-time ambassador of Cajun culture.

Today, Balfa's efforts are obvious to anyone strolling through the famous French Quarter tourist district in New Orleans. Cajun music blasts out of bars, beckoning to tourists and inspiring some to dance in the street. Cajun bands such as Beausoleil, and Steve Riley and the Mamou Playboys have found success, playing concerts across the United States, Europe, and elsewhere. From its humble roots in the Louisiana bayou, the sizzling music of the Cajun people has grown into an international phenomenon.

Rockin' Zydeco

The region where the Cajuns lived was also inhabited by African Americans who, despite rigid segregation, lived little differently than their white neighbors. Black people spoke French, worked long hours as farmers and laborers, and held dances where music was played on accordions, fiddles, washboards, and triangles. Unlike the Cajuns, however, these people, known as Creoles, have a long tradition of

Tejano Music

The players of Cajun and zydeco are not the only musicians to use the accordion to provide enticing dance music. Tex-Mex, or Tejano, music is played by Texans of Mexican heritage who blend elements of Mexican polka, disco, country, and rock.

Tejano originated with old-fashioned conjunto music, which melded romantic love songs (bolero) with songs idealizing rural life (rancha). These were played on the accordion with a one-two, one-two polka beat. In the 1950s, band leader Isidro Lopez merged conjunto with a big band sound using keyboards, a horn section, and electric guitars. The resulting music came to be known as Tejano and, like other forms of regional music, the style has evolved over the years. In the 1970s, accordionist Flaco Jimenez, whose father was a famous conjunto musician, added elements of jazz, blues, and rock to the Tejano sound. In 1990 Jimenez became a member of the Grammy Award–winning Texas Tornadoes supergroup with other Tejano stars such as Freddy Fender and Doug Sahm. Two years later, Selena became the first Tejano star to achieve massive success. Her album *Mi Mundo* eventually sold over a million copies.

Although Selena died tragically, murdered by a fan in 1995, she took Tejano from the Texas border to people across the globe. As a sound that mixes many elements from the American melting pot, Tejano music is a distinct regional sound with an international flavor.

Selena was one of the most popular Tejano, or Tex-Mex, performers.

music dating back to Africa. Their music, known as zydeco, is "a little jazz, a little blues, a little French and a little rhythm 'n' blues, all mixed together,"[59] says accordionist Rockin' Dopsie Jr.

In the 1920s and 1930s, while the Falcons were introducing Cajun music to the world, black accordionists Sidney Babineaux and Adam Fontenot were recording a style, known as *la la* music, with a similar sound. In the 1950s, la la was transformed into zydeco by Clifton Chenier, who recorded over one hundred albums between 1955 and his death in 1987.

Chenier took the la la sound and refashioned it to fit the rocking fifties, putting aside the ten-button accordion for a full-size piano accordion. His brother, Cleveland, remade the washboard, taking a piece of corrugated steel, cutting shoulder harnesses into the metal, and strapping it across his chest. Instead of clacking on this rubboard with a bottle opener in each hand, Cleveland held several openers between each of his fingers. The result of these innovations was a new sound altogether. Grace Lichtenstein and Laura Dankner describe Chenier's style in *Musical Gumbo:*

Imagine a Cajun band—fiddle, accordion, guitar, and triangle. Now subtract the fiddle and substitute a rubboard, which looks like a corrugated metal chest protector. Add a drum kit and perhaps a tenor sax, even a piano. With the accordion pounding out a melody and the other instruments providing an incessant two-step or waltz rhythm, imagine the leader singing an R & B-type fast tune or an old blues number using country, rather than urban, imagery ("I'm a hog for you, baby") in French. That's zydeco.[60]

Chenier's transformation of la la earned him the title King of Zydeco, and he often performed wearing a crown. Following his lead, other black Louisiana musicians rocked up zydeco and took it from New Orleans to the world stage. Boozoo Chavis, Rockin' Dopsie, Buckwheat Zydeco, and John Delafose and the Eunice Playboys have all recorded hits melding zydeco with rock, blues, and Afro-Caribbean dance rhythms. Meanwhile, the undisputed Queen of Zydeco, Queen Ida, has won several Grammy awards and has toured extensively in the United States, Canada, and Europe.

With talented players like Queen Ida and Beausoleil, it is little wonder that zydeco and Cajun tunes are popular from the Louisiana bayous to the musical theaters of Europe. The soulful sounds created within the fifty United States, from the southern border to the Hawaiian Islands, have provided inspiration for musicians on every continent. With its swinging dance beats and irresistible sing-along lyrics, the music of the United States is not just American music but music of the world.

• Notes •

Introduction: Billions of Listeners Worldwide

1. Quoted in Tom Schnabel, *Rhythm Planet: The Great World Music Makers*. New York: Universe, 1998, p. 7.

Chapter One: Music of Southern Africa

2. Quoted in Ruth M. Stone, ed., *The Garland Handbook of African Music*. New York: Garland, 2000, p. 311.
3. Paul F. Berliner, *The Soul of Mbira*. Chicago: University of Chicago Press, 1993, p. 11.
4. Mbira.org, "Shona Mbira Music of Zimbabwe," February 2005. www.mbira.org/index.html.
5. Ronnie Graham, *The Da Capo Guide to Contemporary African Music*. New York: Da Capo, 1988, p. 287.
6. Quoted in Simon Broughton et al., eds., *World Music: The Rough Guide*. London: Rough Guides, 1994, p. 401.
7. Simon Broughton et al., eds., *World Music: The Rough Guide*, p. 373.
8. Billy Bergman, *Goodtime Kings: Emerging African Pop*. New York: Quill, 1985, p. 113.

Chapter Two: Music of West and Central Africa

9. Quoted in Jürgen Streeck, "Historical Sources of Rap: The African-American 'Oral Tradition,'" University of Texas, 2002. www.utexas.edu/coc/cms/faculty/streeck/hiphop/Ancestor_genres.pdf.
10. Bergman, *Goodtime Kings*, p. 99.
11. Quoted in Simon Broughton et al., eds., *World Music Volume 1: Africa, Europe and the Middle East*. London: Rough Guides, 2000, p. 617.
12. Quoted in Broughton et al., eds., *World Music Volume 1*, p. 620.
13. Schnabel, *Rhythm Planet*, p. 103.
14. Quoted in Broughton et al., eds., *World Music Volume 1*, p. 621.
15. Quoted in Schnabel, *Rhythm Planet*, p. 103.
16. Quoted in Broughton et al., eds., *World Music Volume 1*, p. 592.
17. Susan Orlean, "The Congo Sound," *New Yorker*, October 14, 2002. www.newyorker.com/fact/content/?021014fa_fact2.

Chapter Three: Music of North Africa and the Middle East

18. Broughton et al., *World Music: The Rough Guide*, p. 167.
19. Quoted in Schnabel, *Rhythm Planet*, p. 64.
20. Quoted in Broughton et al., eds., *World Music: The Rough Guide*, p. 127.

21. Quoted in Banning Eyre, "Khaled," Afropop Worldwide, 2003. www.afropop.org/explore/artist_info/ID/23/Khaled.
22. Quoted in Schnabel, *Rhythm Planet*, p. 65.
23. Quoted in Schnabel, *Rhythm Planet*, p. 64.
24. Quoted in Broughton et al., eds., *World Music Volume 1*, p. 342.
25. Banning Eyre, "Shaabi," Afropop Worldwide, 2003. www.afropop.org/explore/style_info/ID/6/Shaabi.

Chapter Four: Music of India and the Far East

26. Ravi Shankar, "On Appreciation of Indian Classical Music," Ravi Shankar Foundation, 2000. www.ravishankar.org/indian_music.html.
27. Ravi Shankar, "On Appreciation of Indian Classical Music."
28. Ravi Shankar, "On Appreciation of Indian Classical Music."
29. Quoted in Simon Broughton and Mark Ellingham, eds., *World Music Volume, 2: Latin & North America, Caribbean, India, Asia and Pacific.* London: Rough Guides, 2000, p. 63.
30. Quoted in Broughton and Ellingham, eds., *World Music, Volume 2*, pp. 63–64.
31. Quoted in Jeff Todd Titon, ed., *Worlds of Music.* New York: Schirmer, 1992, p. 213.
32. Don Heckman, "Bollywood's Voice, Onstage and in Person," *Los Angeles Times*, June 21, 2005, p. E3.
33. Chris Nickson, *The NPR Curious Listener's Guide to World Music.* New York: Perigee, 2004, p. 84.

Chapter Five: Celtic Music and the Sounds of Eastern Europe

34. June Skinner Sawyers, *Celtic Music: A Complete Guide.* New York: Da Capo, 2000, p. 6.
35. Geoff Wallis and Sue Wilson, *The Rough Guide to Irish Music.* London: Rough Guides, 2001, p. 163.
36. Quoted in Sawyers, *Celtic Music*, p. 299.
37. Wallis and Wilson, *The Rough Guide to Irish Music*, pp. 150–51.
38. Sawyers, *Celtic Music*, p. 270.
39. Quoted in Broughton et al., *World Music: The Rough Guide*, p. 77.
40. Peter Spencer, *World Beat.* Pennington, NJ: A Cappella, 1992, p. 51.

Chapter Six: Music of the Caribbean

41. Rubén Martinez, "Havana: The Golden Era," PBS: Buena Vista Social Club. www.pbs.org/buenavista/film/introduction.html.
42. Broughton et al., *World Music: The Rough Guide*, p. 476.
43. Ed Morales, *The Latin Beat.* New York: Da Capo, 2003, pp. 5–6.
44. Morales, *The Latin Beat*, pp. 16–17.
45. Mikal Gilmore, "The Life and Times of Bob Marley: How He Changed the World Forever," *Rolling Stone,* March 10, 2005, p. 73.

Chapter Seven: Music of Latin America

46. Quoted in Broughton and Ellingham, *World Music, Volume 2*, p. 274.
47. Quoted in Dale A. Olsen and Daniel E. Sheehy, eds., *The Garland Handbook of Latin American Music*. New York: Garland, 2000, pp. 164–65.
48. Quoted in Broughton and Ellingham, *World Music, Volume 2*, p. 470.
49. Quoted in Titon, *Worlds of Music*, p. 381.
50. Olsen and Sheehy, *The Garland Handbook of Latin American Music*, p. 90.
51. Quoted in Sharna Fabian, "Tango Music," Worldhistory.com, 2005. www.worldhistory.com/wiki/T/Tango-music.htm.
52. Quoted in Peter Fryer, *Rhythms of Resistance*. Hanover, NH: Wesleyan University Press, 2000, p. 134.
53. Quoted in Fryer, *Rhythms of Resistance*, p. 89.
54. Quoted in Broughton and Ellingham, eds., *World Music, Volume 2*, p. 335.
55. Morales, *The Latin Beat*, p. 26.

Chapter Eight: World Music of the United States

56. Floyd Red Crow Westerman, liner notes from *Going Back, Yesterday, Today and Tomorrow*. Red Crow Creations, 2001 CD.
57. Keith Secola, liner notes from *Wild Band of Indians*. Akina, 1996 CD.
58. Quoted in Broughton and Ellingham, eds., *World Music, Volume 2*, p. 600.
59. Quoted in Broughton and Ellingham, eds., *World Music, Volume 2*, p. 619.
60. Grace Lichtenstein and Laura Dankner, *Musical Gumbo*. New York: W.W. Norton, 1993, p. 219.

• For Further Reading •

Books

Andrea Bergamini, *Music of the World*. Hauppauge, NY: Barron's Educational Series, 1999. This volume delves into the music of all the world's cultures and spans the millennia from antiquity to the present day, exploring how music was performed and the roles it played in diverse cultures.

Monica Brown, *My Name Is Celia: The Life of Celia Cruz*. Flagstaff, AZ. Rising Moon, 2004. The Queen of Salsa describes her childhood in Cuba, her musical career, and her move to the United States.

James Haskins, *One Love, One Heart*. New York: Jump at the Sun, 2003. A history of reggae for young adults that focuses on how the music has helped shape the culture, religion, dress, and language of Jamaica.

———, *One Nation Under a Groove: Rap Music and Its Roots*. New York: Jump at the Sun/Hyperion Books for Children, 2000. An interesting examination of the roots of rap in ancient African griot music.

Jeff Todd Titon and Bob Carlin, eds., *American Musical Traditions. Volume 5: Latino American and Asian American Music*. New York: Schirmer Reference, 2002. Published in collaboration with the Smithsonian Folkways Recordings, this book examines the history, styles, and overall impact of music from Latin and Asian people in the United States.

• Works Consulted •

Books

Billy Bergman, *Goodtime Kings: Emerging African Pop.* New York: Quill, 1985. A study of eight African music styles including highlife, soukous, Afro-beat, juju, and others.

Paul F. Berliner, *The Soul of Mbira.* Chicago: University of Chicago Press, 1993. A comprehensive exploration of the music and traditions of the Shona people of Zimbabwe that focuses on the thumb piano, or mbira.

Simon Broughton, Mark Ellingham, David Muddyman, and Richard Trillo, eds., *World Music: The Rough Guide.* London: Rough Guides, 1994. An impressive reference work that spans the music of seventy different countries and regions with musician interviews, lyric translations, reviews, and discographies.

Simon Broughton, Mark Ellingham, and Richard Trillo, eds., *World Music, Volume 1: Africa, Europe and the Middle East.* London: Rough Guides, 2000. An updated version of the *Rough Guide* world music series with expanded coverage given to a greater variety of music from nearly every nation on earth.

Simon Broughton and Mark Elling-ham, eds., *World Music, Volume 2: Latin & North America, Caribbean, India, Asia and Pacific.* London: Rough Guides, 2000. The second volume from Rough Guides' *World Music* series.

Banning Eyre, *In Griot Time.* Philadelphia: Temple University Press, 2000. The story of an American guitarist who spent seven months in Mali, living with native musicians and learning about the history and culture behind the most popular sounds in the world music genre.

Peter Fryer, *Rhythms of Resistance.* Hanover, NH: Wesleyan University Press, 2000. An exploration of the African roots of Brazilian dance and music that encompasses four centuries of slavery, colonization, and indigenous influence.

Ronnie Graham, *The Da Capo Guide to Contemporary African Music.* New York: Da Capo, 1988. A country-by-country overview of music played on the African continent with a summary of regional influences, and biographies and discographies of leading musicians and bands.

Rick Koster, *Louisiana Music.* New York: Da Capo, 2002. Louisiana is home to more styles of music than any other state, and this book details the rise of jazz, blues, ragtime, Cajun, zydeco, gospel, and other styles.

Grace Lichtenstein and Laura Dankner, *Musical Gumbo.* New York: W.W. Norton, 1993. An exploration of Louisiana music from the early days of jazz and R & B to Cajun, zydeco, and modern jazz.

Ed Morales, *The Latin Beat.* New York: Da Capo, 2003. A study of the incredible variety of music from Latin America and how those sounds have transformed music in the United States, Europe, Africa, and elsewhere.

Angela M.S. Nelson, ed., *This Is How We Flow.* Columbia: University of South Carolina Press, 1999. A collection of essays written by scholars and artists concerning African and African American cultural connections in music, religion, literature, art, film, dance, and protest.

Chris Nickson, *The NPR Curious Listener's Guide to World Music.* New York: Perigee, 2004. A concise history of world music with a nation-by-nation guide to styles and stars. The author includes a glossary of world music terms and a list of fifty of the most important world music CDs.

J.H. Kwabena Nketia, *The Music of Africa.* New York: W.W. Norton, 1974. A study of indigenous African music, its historical, cultural, and social background, and the groups and organizations that played it in the decades before the term world music was popularized.

Dale A. Olsen and Daniel E. Sheehy, eds., *The Garland Handbook of Latin American Music.* New York: Garland, 2000. An all-inclusive look at the music of Mexican and Central and South American nations that includes lyrics, sheet music, and details about musical cultures and histories,

June Skinner Sawyers, *Celtic Music: A Complete Guide.* New York: Da Capo, 2000. An exploration of music from Ireland, Scotland, and Wales from its twelfth-century roots to the twenty-first century, in which Celtic music is among the best-selling in the world music market.

Tom Schnabel, *Rhythm Planet: The Great World Music Makers.* New York: Universe, 1998. A series of short biographies of musicians who play world music including well-known players such as Bob Marley, Ruben Blades, Ravi Shankar, and Milton Nascimento.

Peter Spencer, *World Beat.* Pennington, NJ: A Cappella, 1992. A guide to world music that includes performers, reviews, CDs, and resources.

Ruth M. Stone, ed., *The Garland Handbook of African Music.* New York: Garland, 2000. A selection of essays written by leading music scholars concerning many aspects of African music; includes a CD and regional case studies from all regions of the continent.

Jeff Todd Titon, ed., *Worlds of Music.* New York: Schirmer, 1992. An exploration of the musical styles of Native Americans, Africans, eastern Europeans, Indians, Asians, and others, presented in the context of human life and culture.

Dave Thompson, *Reggae & Caribbean Music.* San Francisco: Backbeat, 2002. A comprehensive book covering the regional music from Trinidad to Barbados; includes musical history, artists' biographies, CD reviews, and photos.

Geoff Wallis and Sue Wilson, *The Rough Guide to Irish Music.* London: Rough Guides, 2001. A comprehensive guide to Irish music with historical background, biographical entries, discographies, and lists of the most recent trends and popular artists in Ireland.

Periodicals

Mikal Gilmore, "The Life and Times of Bob Marley: How He Changed the World Forever," *Rolling Stone*, March 10, 2005.

Don Heckman, "Bollywood's Voice, Onstage and in Person," *Los Angeles Times,* June 20, 2005.

Internet Sources

Keola Beamer, "A Brief History of Slack Key Guitar," mauimapp.com, June 28, 2005: www.mauimapp. com/moolelo.htm.

CaribPlanet, "Caribbean Music 101: Soca," July 7, 2001. http://caribplanet. homestead.com/101_Soca.html.

Eric Charry, "West African Music," Wesleyan University Music De-

partment, January 23, 2002. http:// echarry.web.wesleyan.edu/Afmus. html.

Drummerworld, "Airto Moreira." www. drummerworld.com/drummers/Airt o_Moreira.html.

Banning Eyre, "Balla Tounkara, The Griot of Boston," Afropop Worldwide, August 2000. www.afropop. org/multi/feature/ID/10.

———, "Khaled," Afropop Worldwide, 2003. www.afropop.org/ explore/artist_info/ID/23/Khaled.

———, "Shaabi," Afropop Worldwide, 2003. www.afropop.org/explore/ style_info/ID/6/Shaabi.

Sharna Fabian, "Tango Music," Worldhistory.com, 2005. www.worldhis tory.com/wiki/T/Tango-music.htm.

Victor Jara, "Chile Stadium" in "Latin American Music: Culture and Politics," North Carolina State University. http://social.chass.ncsu.edu/ slatta/hi216/music.htm.

Rubén Martinez, "Havana: The Golden Era," PBS: Buena Vista Social Club. www.pbs.org/buenavista/ film/introduction.html.

Susan Orlean, "The Congo Sound," *New Yorker*, October 14, 2002. www.newyorker.com/fact/con tent/?021014fa_fact2.

Anoushka Shankar, "Anoushka Shankar: Biography" May 2005. www. anoushkashankar.com.

Ravi Shankar, "On Appreciation of Indian Classical Music," Ravi Shankar Foundation, 2000. www. ravishankar.org/indian_music.html.

Jürgen Streeck, "Historical Sources of

Rap: The African-American 'Oral Tradition'," University of Texas, 2002. www.utexas.edu/coc/cms/faculty/streeck/hiphop/Ancestor_genres.pdf.

Other Sources

Keith Secola, liner notes from *Wild Band of Indians*. Akina, 1996, CD. An album by the Anishinabe singer and songwriter.

Floyd Red Crow Westerman, liner notes from *Going Back, Yesterday, Today and Tomorrow*. Red Crow Creations, 2001, CD. An album containing two previous releases, *Custer Died for Your Sins* and *The Land Is Your Mother*.

• Index •

• Picture Credits •

Cover: © Reuters/CORBIS

• About the Author •

Stuart A. Kallen is the author of more than two hundred nonfiction books for children and young adults. He has written on topics ranging from the theory of relativity to the history of rock and roll. In addition, Mr. Kallen has written award-winning children's videos and television scripts. In his spare time, Stuart A. Kallen is a singer, songwriter, and guitarist in San Diego, California.